NASHVILL
MY LIFE IN COUNTRY MUSIC

DON DAVIS
AS TOLD TO RUTH B. WHITE

4880 Lower Valley Road • Atglen, PA 19310

Cover image: A Grand Ole Opry Show sponsored by Royal Crown Cola. The theme song, sung by the band every Saturday night was:

Swing your partner round and round
Right foot up and left foot down
When you think thirsty, drink a Royal Crown
Turkey in the straw, turkey in the hay
Royal Crown Cola every single day

Schiffer Books are available at special discounts for bulk purchases for sales promotions or premiums. Special editions, including personalized covers, corporate imprints, and excerpts can be created in large quantities for special needs. For more information contact the publisher:

Published by Schiffer Publishing, Ltd.
4880 Lower Valley Road
Atglen, PA 19310
Phone: (610) 593-1777; Fax: (610) 593-2002
E-mail: Info@schifferbooks.com

For the largest selection of fine reference books on this and related subjects,
please visit our website at **www.schifferbooks.com**
You may also write for a free catalog.

This book may be purchased from the publisher.
Please try your bookstore first.

We are always looking for people to write books on new and related subjects.
If you have an idea for a book,
please contact us at *proposals@schifferbooks.com*

Schiffer Books are available at special discounts for bulk purchases for sales promotions or premiums. Special editions, including personalized covers, corporate imprints, and excerpts can be created in large quantities for special needs. For more information contact the publisher.

In Europe, Schiffer books are distributed by
Bushwood Books
6 Marksbury Ave.
Kew Gardens
Surrey TW9 4JF England
Phone: 44 (0) 20 8392 8585; Fax: 44 (0) 20 8392 9876
E-mail: info@bushwoodbooks.co.uk
Website: www.bushwoodbooks.co.uk

Designed by Mark David Bowyer

Type set in CM Old Western / Zurich BT

ISBN: 978-0-7643-4279-0
Printed in China

CONTENTS

DEDICATION

To all the musicians who beat those roads with their bass fiddles in the car or tied on top, and the steel guitar players whose guitars and amps had to be lifted to the top. To all those who sweated it out on two-lane roads, with no air conditioning, and traveled miles promoting the Grand Ole Opry and country music.

The Country Music Association (CMA) should certainly recognize all these musicians, and it could be so simple: just collect the names of the musicians, put them into a station set-up with a short biography, and then their names could be brought up to be read on the screen to be seen by interested persons.

Somebody, somewhere, knows every one of these old boys. The stars couldn't have done their acts "*a cappella*." They needed these good-old boys to back them up while doing their acts.

—Donald S. Davis

FOREWORD

Don Davis and I go back further than most of the musicians here today. The very first session I ever played on was with Pee Wee King in Chicago in 1946 for RCA. I was the extra guy. Pee Wee had Red Stewart with him who played guitar and fiddle, but we recorded "direct to disc" in those days. There was no such thing as "overdubbing." Red couldn't play both instruments at the same time, so I was hired to play guitar on that session. Don was the steel guitar player. He played amazingly well.

After that session, I took two weeks off from college and went to Texas with Pee Wee and the band. I remember that one of the dates was at the Huntsville State Prison Rodeo. Don and I and the band all got sunburned watching the convicts riding those horses.

Nashville was beginning to be a presence in the record industry when Castle Studios opened at the Tulane Hotel. There is no telling how many sessions Don and I did there. We played the first notes ever played at Castle.

All of us were so young then. Don and Grady Martin used to go "roaring" together. They would get in fights at a place in East Nashville called the Glenview Inn. Don would wake up the next morning, all bruised and battered, and say, "Hey, they told me I was winning that fight!" We all laughed at Don's antics. He had a great sense of humor and anyone around him had a lot of great laughs along the way.

Hank Garland was one of Nashville's great guitar players. One day his brother, Billy, brought me a jazz album that Hank and Don had played on, and Don was so good on it. It was an exceptional album. Don was just as much at home playing jazz as he was playing country.

Don played a key role in this city's rise as a recording center following World War II. As the Music City gained in fame, his work as a musician, producer, artist manager, and publisher was at the heart of the music industry. He had an uncanny sense of finding the right song for an artist. For instance, three of Johnny Cash's hits were discovered by Don. He was an excellent musician, a great player, an exceptionally good steel player and the records he played on prove it.

—Harold Bradley

Harold Bradley was President of Local 257, Nashville Musicians' Union; Vice President of the International Musicians' Union; an inductee of the Country Music Hall Of Fame; and was the first president of the National Academy of Recording Arts & Sciences (NARAS). In 1955, he and his brother, Owen Bradley, built the first recording studio on Music Row. Harold is the world's most recorded guitar player. In 2010, he received the prestigious Grammy Trustees' award.

PREFACE

It all began some four score years ago here in Mobile. And now here I am again. It's been a long hard ride from Mobile to Nashville, points in between, and back again, but I loved my life then and I love my life now. I'm truly a satisfied man. As I sit on the sands here beside the bay, I often think, "Where is the life that late I led, when each day was filled with the sound of music?"

My family scratched out a bare existence and I know I was damn lucky to have made it in the music business. I was fiercely independent, one of a hearty breed of southern Alabamians who reached for the stars and eventually made it. It seems impossible to me that, at 16 years old, I got my first look at the big time when Pee Wee King hired me as his steel player. I can laugh now when I think of the people who laughed at my kind of music by saying, "Oh, well, he plays 'Hillbilly' Music!" I wonder now, "When did they stop calling it hillbilly and begin using the term 'country'?" Then came the rockers and the outlaws, and I was part of it all.

The waves keep coming in, and in my imagination, in each wave I see the faces of so many artists, musicians, and songwriters with whom I've worked: Pee Wee, George Morgan, Ernest Tubb, The Carter Family, Chet Atkins, Harlan Howard, Hank Williams, and so many more, all gone now. I think about the good times I've shared with these people and one incident I recall makes me smile, that of Johnny Cash, the man in black.

When I first met Johnny Cash, he had not yet become a legend or married June Carter. When he married June, he became my brother-in-law, as I was married to Anita Carter, June's sister. Many hits later, the image of the "man in black" and a free and swinging lifestyle all projected him into the category of a legend. Fans became fascinated with his outlaw image, the alcohol, drugs, run-ins with the law, and his road antics. Of course, to me he was just a great talent, capable of having hits. What the fans didn't know was that Johnny had his ups and downs with Columbia Records.

So, when Shel Silverstein, a well known song writer and author, came into my office at Wilderness Publishing Co. and played and sang me a song he had written on his old guitar, I knew immediately the only person who could cut it was Johnny Cash. The song was "A Boy Named Sue." I knew Johnny needed a hit song at that time, so I called him and said, "John, I know you get a lot of songs and I wouldn't bother you if I didn't know you'd want this song. It's called 'A Boy Named Sue.' Shel Silverstein wrote it." John said, "Bring it out now."

The song wasn't even demo-ed, so when I took Shel out to John's house, he sang it to him live. When we left, all John had was the lyrics.

This happened to be the day before John and June were leaving for San Quentin. When they left the next day, John would have left the lyrics at home if June had not reminded him to take them along. While he was performing at San Quentin, he laid the lyrics down on the floor in front of him. There had been no time for rehearsal.

He told his audience, "I have a new song. I don't know it yet, but I'll sing it for you the best I can." John just talked it while the band chorded behind him. It was a talkin' blues kind of a song and was easy to follow. The prisoners went crazy when they heard it. It was an instant hit.

When Columbia released his next album, which included "A Boy Named Sue" recorded live at San Quentin, it made Johnny Cash the biggest selling artist in 1969. The single stayed at number one for five weeks.

I was proud of my part in getting the song to Cash; and Harlan Howard and I, at Wilderness, didn't even have publishing on it. It belonged to Evil Eye Music. However, there came a day when a silver lining appeared in the sky. Shel showed back up at the office one day and brought me a check for $7200, part of his royalty check. Not many writers would have done that. But the biggest thrill of all was having found a hit for Johnny Cash. I don't think anything I ever did in the music business could top the high you get when Johnny Cash has a hit song you pitched to him.

As I sit here day-dreaming, sifting the sand between my fingers, it occurs to me that I need to put all my fun times and sad times down on paper, my life as a musician and as a businessman. That life took me all the way to Nashville from Mobile, from California to New York and back again. I guess I've been everywhere. I've played in some big towns and heard the big boys talk. I've played in some small towns and talked to just plain folks. I've heard bad songs, some good songs, and a few great songs. These are now all precious memories, but I was there when it happened, when Nashville became Music City, USA. I worked with the stars and legends when they were hot and sometimes when they cooled down. I also was there when they said their last good-byes. And now? Well, I was there when it began and now I'm ready to talk. Here's my story, from the beginning.

—Don Davis

ACKNOWLEDGMENTS

I am indebted to the artists, associates, friends, and family of Don Davis who have given of their time and thoughts to this project.

So many of the musicians, artists and songwriters discussed in this book have passed away, but they live forever in our memories, so our thanks go out to them for their long ago participation in this business we call music. Don's daughter, Lorrie Davis Bennett, and his wife, Serilda Davis, both of whom know the real Don Davis, gave their honest opinions of this very funny and talented man.

I want to give special thanks to Harold Bradley, who was generous in giving me his time and insightful approach to his long time "brother" in the Nashville Musicians' Union.

I can always count on the encouragement and knowledge of Walt Trott, editor of the *Nashville Musician*, and on Dick Hill, a Nebraska musician and historian who generously shared his info on Cowboy Slim Rinehart,

Thanks to Jeannie Seely, one of a kind, who allowed us to use her quote which so aptly suits Don's way of thinking.

Although the musicians all said, "What a character," they added to a lot of the stories told here. There was Ray Edenton, Billy Robinson, Floyd Robinson, Bud Isaacs, Lucille Starr, Don Slayman, Barney Miller, Howard White, and Bobbe Seymour. And thanks to Bobby Moore, who never finished a great story. D. Kilpatrick and Joe Johnson, producers, added to our knowledge of recording stories. Songwriters John Riggs and Lola Jean Dillon were ready and willing to give us their memories of a time gone by. Thanks also to a former Sho Bud employee, Leslie Elliott, who laughed her way through an impromptu interview at TGI Fridays; and to Dr. Nat Winston, who laughed as we discussed Don, Anita, and a lion.

I had a great phone interview with Gene Ferguson, Artist Manager and Promoter, who was on the scene when Cash recorded "One Piece at a Time." He told me to write the story, just as Don told me.

Wayne Grove's knowledge of coins proved of great value. James "Shortdog" Martin always comes through when I need help defining his community. This time he found Jesse McAdoo, who lived with Good Jelly Jones for nine years.

It was so pleasant talking with Mrs. Alveda Newman, who has lived in Mom Upchurch's house since Mom died.

I appreciate Billy Ray Reynolds calling me from Mississippi to tell me, in his way, of how he acquired a Daland Guitar.

Thanks also to my daughter, "Kat," for her great insight into music. She gave me the line, "Back when it was all about the music."

Howard White, a former Grand Ole Opry steel player who worked for Davis at Wilderness Music, deserves special thanks for driving "Miss Ruth" to Gulf Shores over and over for meetings with Davis and to the interviews with the famous and not so famous. Howard passed to his place of "perfect tranquility" in 2008. Don and I miss our best promoter.

Both Davis and I thank the U.S. Postal Service for getting our tapes and mail back and forth so promptly. I am grateful Don gave me the opportunity to join with him in this story of his creative life.

—Ruth White, Gallatin, Tennessee

"Maybe that wasn't the way it was, but they're my memories and I'll remember them the way I want to."

—Jeannie Seely, from the Grand Ole Opry

PART ONE
LIFE IN MOBILE

They saw a swallow building his nest,
I guess they figured he knew best,
So they built a town around him
And they called it Mobile.

—Wells/Holt

Chapter 1
JUST A FIGHTIN' ALABAMA BOY

In 1928, Herbert Hoover was elected president of the United States. On the 22nd of December, 1928, I was born in Calvert, Washington County, Alabama, just across the line from Mobile County. I made it ten months before the Depression hit. You see, even then, I didn't want to miss a thing. There certainly was nothing "roaring" about the 1920s in Calvert. Folks were too busy trying to make a living. They were damn lucky just to make ends meet. In fact, the whole financial situation in Alabama at that time could be called depressing.

I was born in the home of my aunt and uncle, the Patricks, where we were living at the time. My mom, Annabelle Patrick Davis, and my dad, Buster Davis, separated right after I was born. We were poor, but I didn't know it, because everybody I knew was poor. My uncle worked for the Works Progress Administration (WPA) and made $1.25 a day. People used to joke and call it the Worker's Piddler Association, or "We Piddle Around." I was kinda raised up with my two first cousins, Anita Dean and Bebe. I called them my sisters. I went to first grade at Calvert School.

Don Davis,
three years old.

Don Davis, five years old.

My father moved to Detroit, Michigan, to live with his mother, my grandmother. Shortly after, before my mother re-married, I also moved to my grandmother's in Detroit. I was about 7 years old and in the second grade at Fitzgerald School. I lived at 15492 North Lawn, just off Woodward Avenue, a very popular street in an upper middle-class neighborhood.

My father worked at Marathon Tire Co. He was what they called a "combination mechanic," that is, he re-grooved tires and did front-end alignments, and engine diagnosis. (There was no electronic equipment to assist the mechanic in those days.) When I was a little boy, I went to work with him one day and watched him re-groove tires, a real tedious job. They had a tool that would take the tires, after the tread was worn down, and re-groove them. You had to be real careful. If you got too deep you would go into the cord. There was a real art to that. Times were still bad and everybody tried to save as much money as they could. They could afford to buy tires that had already been re-grooved or they could have the tires already on their car re-grooved.

My father drove like a maniac. He also had a thing about panel trucks. He loved panel trucks. The company had one and he drove it a lot. He was fond of a little 1935 Pontiac coupe that he owned. I remember that I'd see him when he was going to work and he'd hammer down and take the corner on two wheels when he'd leave. One of the things I can remember him saying was, "The accelerator and the brake should be connected together so when you take your foot off the gas, it puts on the brakes." He firmly believed that's the way a car should be designed. You'd either go or stop. He was reckless. I remember going out to a track that a guy had designed for a hobby and watching my father in that '35 Pontiac go up on a ramp that turned the car up on two wheels, like they used to do at thrill shows. Lucky Teeter, a famous thrill driver, had a Plymouth that he used to thrill audiences that way at fairs and the like.

My father married a woman from Greenwood Springs, Mississippi, named Efenia. He moved down there and not long after died from appendicitis.

I was still living with my grandmother when she became ill with cancer. In her final days, my step-grandfather, William Adair, called my mother and told her the situation there. She told him she had re-married and I could go back to Alabama with her. So I rode the train from Detroit down to Mobile. I was only 9 years old, but in those days Traveler's Aid took care of kids. You were registered with them and they had somebody at every stop to look after you 'till you reached your destination.

My mother was married to J.C. Beard. Everybody called him "Jiggs" because he looked like Jiggs in the comic strip "Maggie And Jiggs."

I called him "Papa Jiggs." They picked me up at the train station in a Model A Ford. I'll never forget that. You see, I was used to a big car in Detroit. My step grandfather worked for James J. Bright & Wood, a big auto service company. He was the service manager, and he and my grandmother had a thing about Hudsons. They bought a new Hudson every year and I was used to riding around in those fancy cars. So to suddenly ride in a Model A Ford was like riding in a puddle jumper.

My mother and Papa Jiggs had a nice rented house in Satsuma, a suburb of Mobile. I was enrolled right away at Satsuma School. When I first came back, I had picked up a Yankee accent. I immediately started getting in fights at school as some of the kids made snide remarks about the way I talked. I got the reputation at an early age as a scrapper. I bloodied a few noses until my accent gradually went away.

Satsuma School was almost like a consolidated school because kids from all the little country towns around there, such as Creola, were all bused in there to school. With all those kids from different areas, it didn't take me long to make friends. I mean, to make friends you had to kick ass. They didn't respect you until you fought them. Once you did, you were a fine dude. So I started off real good! Then the teachers started sending notes home to my mother about my fighting on school grounds. It got to be a serious problem, I guess, as my mother tried to talk to me about it.

By that time I had become pretty well attached to Papa Jiggs. I really liked him. I was never mistreated. My mother said to him, "J.C., I want you to talk to Donald about this note here about his fighting on school grounds. It's the second or third time they've sent one." "Well," Papa Jiggs said, "I'll talk to him about it." So we went outside and had a little confidential conversation. "Now, Moon," he said, (using the nickname he had given me because, he said, the moon affected my mind. Whenever I acted up he'd tell me, "Oh, oh, the tide is nipping!") He paused, got quiet and thoughtful, then said, "I want you to quit fighting on school grounds. Wait until you get off the school grounds." I'll never forget that. He came from up in Choctaw County and went to school at Silas, Alabama, and played football up there. In a way, he was a little bit proud that I was a fighter. He didn't tell me to quit fighting, he just said don't fight on the school grounds.

There was an old gravel road from the school to our house, Old Highway 43, across from the new highway. A railroad track ran between them with a ditch along side. There was water in the ditch, so one of my buddies and I put old tires in the ditch and catfish would get in the tires. It was a prize thing to catch these little fish. One day I caught some boys from Baker Road, on the other side of the tracks, messing with my catfish and tires. I tangled with them there on the tracks. Papa Jiggs was driving down the gravel road from the store and saw me fighting with the boys. He stopped and said, "You all right, Moon?" I said, "Yeah," and went back to fighting again. He drove on. He just checked to see if I was all right.

I had a little neighbor up on the corner named Marvin Goodman. He was twelve years old, but he was a little bitty guy with arms that looked like pipe stems, red hair, and a freckled face. One day I saw those three boys from Baker Road messing with my tires again. And I yelled at them. They yelled back, "What ya gonna do about it!" And I yelled, "I told ya what I was gonna do about it!" There were three of them, and I'm thinking to myself, "I can't back down. I'm gonna get me one more butt kicking today. I mean I'm really gonna get it. Sure don't look good."

Then Marvin showed up to help me. "Let's go get 'em," he said. That little dude tore into one of them, jumped on him, started clawing his eyes and chewing his ear. He whipped two of them before I could get to one. I mean he tore into them like a buzz saw. After Marvin whipped the two, they all took off running. That third one took off before I got to him. That was a cool experience. The last time I ever saw them, they were running down Baker Road, shirt tails a'flying. I had befriended Marvin because I actually had been afraid somebody might hurt him. He didn't need any help.

Papa Jiggs worked at the International Paper Co., making $9 a week. We had plenty of everything. We were among the elite in the area, because he had that job down at the paper company. Most people didn't have a job. He was even able to trade that Model A Ford in for a 1934 Ford.

Five miles away, in Chickasaw, Alabama, was a supermarket. It was family-owned. When we went there we had to take the back seat out of the car to have enough room for the groceries—about $3 worth. Flour came in 24-pound sacks and you would buy a stand of lard. My mother was a great cook. She used to buy tripe in a large can. Tripe is part of the lining of the stomach of a cow, a white meat but grainy, like leather, but she battered that stuff up and fried it. It would be so tender you could cut it with a fork. It was delicious. We also ate a lot of those big lima beans. My favorite uncle said that the guy who invented penicillin didn't save any lives. The guy who invented those lima beans, he's the one who saved lives. Everybody ate them, sometimes three times a day.

I spent my summers with my Aunt Daisy and Uncle Bossy. They had seven boys and two girls. Uncle Bossy was in the timber business and was on the road most of the time, so Aunt Daisy had to manage their home, a small farm, and their tribe, including me in the summertime. I have great memories of those times. Us boys used to play in the woods and would end up being full of ticks: seed ticks, dog ticks, deer ticks—you name them. Aunt Daisy would make us strip off when we came in from playing, then get out a gallon can of kerosene and wash us down good. Sure killed those ticks! Aunt Daisy had a pie safe and she kept left-over biscuits in there. I'd slip in, get a biscuit or two, punch a hole in the top and pour in syrup. Boy, they were good! With nine or ten of us around, Aunt Daisy had her own brand of discipline. She had a six-foot Gallberry limb, I referred to as a "jump butt." Aunt Daisy became a psychiatrist, hearing specialist, and faith healer all rolled into one. Her jump butt would improve your hearing about ninety per cent in less than five minutes. She knew exactly where to apply that Gallberry limb to get the desired results. She had an upswing that I refer to as the "nerve stroke." When applied to the lower part of the buttocks, it always hit a nerve that adjusted to all the other nerves in the body. It completely changed your attitude. If you tried to fake an illness to avoid chores, like filling up the wood box, that Gallberry limb became a faith healer.

However, there was so much love in that house you forgot the jump butt. There was plenty of food on the table and we all roamed the woods playing, when our chores were done. When I think of the unruly juveniles of today, and that no one is allowed to blister their butts, I always think of Aunt Daisy's Gallberry limb. If our modern day young delinquents were given a little love and pampering, with a little touch of Aunt Daisy's Gallberry limb, it might change their attitude. I keep thinking that if the U.S.A. would enact laws in favor of using the jump butt, I would buy land and raise enough Gallberry limbs to supply the country.

For the uninitiated, let me explain that the Gallberry is a genus of the Laurel family of evergreen shrubs. They grow rampant in Mississippi. One town, Laurel, was built on a Gallberry flat and was named for the Laurel shrubs that grew there. They were poisonous to their cattle so the locals kept them hacked down. Those Gallberry limbs hurt me just as much as they hurt the cattle, I think.

I was in love with my fifth grade teacher, Miss Golden. She was about twenty-two and beautiful. I wanted her for my very own. Recently I wrote her a note and told her about this. I used to stand in front of a mirror and practice my wink so I could flirt with her in the hall. I told her, "Finally I met you in the hall, but my wink froze up on me and all I could do was give you a silly grin." That made her so happy.

They named a school for her and had a dedication ceremony. She invited me to come to it and I did. She was in a wheel chair, but people were lined up just to speak to her: It was a big, beautiful school and I was so proud for her.

That was my life until I graduated from the seventh grade at Satsuma School.

Chapter 2
Ship Building and Country Music

The name of my home state, Alabama, is like magic. So many songs have been written about it, for instance, "Alabama Jubilee," "Alabama Bound," "Stars Fell On Alabama," "Alabam'," and even "Sweet Home Alabama." The name came from a tribe of Indians of the Creek Confederacy who called themselves the "Alibamu," meaning, "I clear the thicket."

The United States captured Mobile from the Spanish in 1813, but the most talked-about battle for Mobile was during the War Between The States (The Civil War), when a Union naval squadron, under Admiral David G. Farragut, sailed into its fortified Southern harbor. Farragut was warned that the harbor bristled with mines, called "torpedoes" in those days. "Damn the torpedoes, full speed ahead," Farragut yelled and roared on. The union did not occupy Mobile, but they completely blockaded it. This closed the last open Confederate port to shipping in their much-needed supplies from England. Mobile was the last Southern stronghold to surrender to the Union force at the end of the War.

Shipbuilding became the important industry in Mobile, continuing even during World War I. When the Depression began in Alabama, many in the state suffered under financial setbacks. More than sixty Alabama banks failed between 1929 and 1931. But the times, they were a'changing. On December 7, 1941, when Pearl Harbor was attacked, it drove the United States into World War II, which affected all the lives in Mobile, Alabama, as well as the rest of the country. Alabama greatly expanded its production to meet Allied needs for munitions, ships, iron, and steel products. Mobile again served as a center for building ships.

I started the eighth grade at Murphy School in Mobile, eighteen miles from Satsuma. Because of the war, there were no buses and no other way to get to school. Gas and tires were rationed. I didn't finish the eighth grade, but while I was there I learned to read blueprints. I applied for a job and got it at Gulf Shipbuilding in Chickasaw, Alabama. With the war on, they needed men to work and fill the contracts they had. I was a minor, but they asked for and got permission from the Child Welfare Department for me to work there as a pipe layout specialist. I was in for some really big bucks at the shipyards, sixty-six cents an hour.

At the same time, Hank Williams was working at Alabama Drydock and Shipbuilding Co. (ADSC). He was a shipfitter's helper and later entered the welder training program. He worked there, on and off, from 1942 until 1944. I didn't meet him then, but people talked about how he wanted to be a country singer and all reports say he was broke and disgusted. He and a friend, Freddie Beech, drove around to the clubs at night and sometimes worked with a band on radio. Audrey Sheppard

Guy (later Mrs. Hank Williams) also spent time there, working side-by-side with him welding ship parts. Then Audrey decided to get a band together for Hank, go back to Montgomery, get a radio show, and start working shows. Hank was making about the same thing I did. He quit his job at ADSC and became the greatest artist and song writer of his day.

By the time I got the job at the shipbuilding company, like Hank, I was already infected with country music, the steel guitar, and the Grand Ole Opry. It seems the shipbuilding industry had hired two of us who couldn't wait for the right time to be able to "pick" full time. One of my buddies from Satsuma had an older brother who had a guitar, just a regular acoustic model. I had been putting old pieces of bicycles together and had made myself a bicycle out of parts. With the war on, you couldn't buy bicycles. Now that guy wanted my bicycle and I wanted his guitar—BAD. That boy, last name Horton, still had that guitar and he still wanted my bicycle, so I swapped that bicycle for his guitar.

The school in Satsuma built a little auditorium. They hired a country band called "Tex Dunn and the Virginia Hillbillies." Tex had a steel guitar player named Gile Gordon with an electric Hawaiian steel guitar. It looked like it had been made out of a door step. He had a little amplifier and the band used his amp for a sound system. They had a microphone they plugged right into it. Tex played the D28 guitar, the first I had ever seen. He made those bass string runs on that thing like Cowboy Slim Rinehart. I had heard Rinehart beaming out from XERA in Mexico, playing his theme song, "I'm A Rovin' Cowboy" and playing these beautiful bass runs on his Martin guitar. As Tex played those beautiful bass runs on his Martin guitar it really inspired me. (Rinehart was inducted into the Texas Country Music Association Hall of Fame in 1996.)

Tex also had a fiddle player named Hal Smith. He was billed as the "Fiddlin' Fool from Fiddlersville." I had heard Hal on the radio. He later played fiddle with stars like Ernest Tubb, but Hal became an icon when, in 1959, he and Ray Price went into the music publishing business with a company called Pamper Music. They attracted Harlan Howard, Hank Cochran, and Willie Nelson, who all became great writers while at Pamper.

I'd heard about a guy that was teaching Hawaiian guitar, George Hazard, charging one dollar a lesson. He came by the house and gave me a little nut to go under the strings of my regular guitar. It raised the strings and then I had a Hawaiian guitar. He gave me two lessons.

He had this number system that showed the string numbers. I learned the first lesson—tune. The next week he came back for the second lesson and I learned that tune. He came back the third week, but I had been listening to the radio and I taught myself a bunch of tunes. When I played for him he told my mom, "I can't teach him anything." So that was it! I took two lessons, so I guess I'm an educated steel guitar player. I did have lessons by a teacher.

Chapter 3
PAY DIRT

My mom and Papa Jiggs moved out of their rented house and bought a house. We had electricity, but no wall sockets. My parents mail ordered a Sears Roebuck electric steel guitar for me that cost $39.95. That included an amplifier with a giant, six-inch speaker. There was a drop cord for a light on the front porch. I took the bulb out, screwed in an adapter plug and plugged my guitar and amp into it. I sat out there and played. The amp didn't have a volume control, I just used the one on the guitar. Cows in the neighboring pastures used to come to the fence and listen. When the cows got out one day, the neighbors complained about the racket I was making. Of course, when I got to Nashville, all of those neighbors claimed they were the ones that got me started. Soon, I learned that the guitar I was playing wasn't too swift. I went down to Mobile to a music store and found a Gibson steel guitar, shaped like a guitar. I bought it and a Gibson amplifier.

By that time, Tex Dunn, who had inspired me, was no longer around, but there were several groups that were what I call semi-pro bands that worked at the shipyards. With the war on, there were several housing projects in Mobile to house defense workers (these places are slums now, but then they were nice). They all had a community center or an auditorium and each Saturday night I played with different bands.

I had a gold-colored nylon shirt and my steel guitar, so I was demanding and got $1.75 a night for these gigs. Since I had so much to offer, I didn't feel like I should cheapen myself by appearing for less than $1.75 a night. After all, nobody but me had a gold-colored nylon shirt!

I was making a killing, working at the shipyards for sixty-six cents an hour by day and making $1.75 a night with a local band, although we usually played only on Saturday nights. Any kind of live entertainment would fill the house. People paid a dime to get in.

This was going fine until I played for a guy I'll call "Red," who had a little band. I would not come off of my $1.75 a night so he fired me after a dance at Alabama Village. He hired another guitar player at $1.50. So he saved twenty-five cents! It was all about the money.

I hit pay dirt the next day. Charley Sailors came by my house and told me he had a touring group and offered me a job with a guarantee of $7 a night. I called the superintendent at the shipyard and told him what he could do with the job long before Johnny Paycheck was ever heard of. (Paycheck's song was "Take This Job And Shove It.")

I found out that Charley's touring group meant touring on the "Kerosene Circuit." These venues consisted of school houses in rural areas that did not have electricity, which meant two things. The rooms were lighted with kerosene lamps and my electric steel guitar was out.

I had to use a flat-top Gene Autry guitar that I modified to Hawaiian style. The only place to do a show was in the classroom. After you left, you could always tell where you had picked because the chalk on the blackboard would be on the seat of your pants.

Charley was quite a showman. He had all kind of gimmicks to draw people. He advertised our show as "Grand Ole Opry Style." It was hyped on placards that had "Grand Ole Opry" in big block letters and underneath it in small letters was "Style." They also said, "See Charley play the guitar with his toes." (He did.) He played "Yankee Doodle" in that manner. I was advertised as the "Wizard Of The Steel Guitar." Other musicians also had exotic titles.

Then Charley got the bright idea of starting a tent show. He rented a stake body, two-ton truck and bought some tarps, posts, concrete blocks and some two-by-something boards for seats. Since tent shows were the big thing, (Barnum and Bailey and even Roy Acuff had them), we were in high cotton. Just one problem: our tent did not have a top. We only had side walls. You couldn't play if it rained. We set up on a vacant lot with a house next door and ran an extension cord from the tent to the house for electricity. We packed 'em in! We played all over Mobile County, Baldwin County, Choctaw County, and all surrounding areas that had a wide spot in the road or a vacant lot (with a house next door). People showed up from all over just to see a live show. There was no TV then. There was no radio reaching the area except WSM and the Grand Ole Opry on Saturday nights.

We ended our tour in lower Alabama (L.A.) and moved to Pelzer, South Carolina, where Charley's mother lived, just outside of Greenville. We moved into her house. His brother, Clarence, worked with us. Clarence played a bass and did a black-face act using burnt cork. He had seen "Jamup and Honey," a vaudeville and Opry minstrel-type act, and thought he could do that. Being a bass player, he was also the comedian. He told jokes and slapped his dog-house bass. ("Dog-house" is what we hillbillies called an "up-right" bass.) That bass sure gave us enough trouble packing it into or on top of cars before the days of buses. It was an important instrument in any band. We didn't use drums in those days, it was the bass that defined the rhythm. Today we use both drums and bass with equal importance.

Charley rented U-Drive-It trucks. That was our mode of transportation. He and his wife sat up front and us guys stood in the back of that damn truck. We'd drive through a town before the show, getting ready to set up. I'd laugh really loud like Oswald on the Grand Ole Opry. Pete Beacher Ray Kirby was known as "Bashful Brother Oswald," who played dobro and sang with Roy Acuff. He was known for his humorous loud laugh and I tried to copy him. I'd yell, "Hey-'ey-'ey, Hey-'ey-'ey, come to the big show tonight. Hey-'ey-'ey!"

I did all this for seven dollars a night! I really began thinking there might be something better than working in a topless tent, ballyhooing the show from the back of the truck, playing with an act that played guitar with his toes and another who played a black-faced act. Well, a musician can dream, can't he?

PART TWO
LIFE IN NASHVILLE

I have roamed this whole world over
Been contented and care free,
When I hear an old time love song,
I think I'm down in Nashville, Tennessee.

—Copas/Monk

Chapter 4

I MAKE THE BIG TIME

In early 1945, I heard that Pee Wee King was going to appear in Asheville, North Carolina, so I went to see him. After the show, I went backstage and met Clell Summey (Cousin Jody). He had an electric guitar, shaped like a guitar except it had a hollow body and a hole so you could play and practice on it without it being plugged in. Clell let me play that thing "raw," in other words "acoustically." That's how I came to meet Pee Wee King. He came over to us and I told him right quick that I would be interested in playing with the Golden West Cowboys, his band. He said that he was aware of me and that he was expecting Clell to be drafted into the army and told me to keep in touch. With that there was hope for something better for this picker.

When we had played the South Carolina area dry, I had no other choice but to go back to Mobile with Charley. That's when I wrote Pee Wee and sent a picture of myself in a cowboy hat and a western scarf. "Remember me?" I wrote, "I played Clell's guitar backstage in Asheville that time." I got a letter back that said, "Meet us in Waycross, Georgia. Clell has been drafted." And that's where I would start with Pee Wee and the band. I never looked back. I took a little satchel packed with my other shirt and clean underwear, my guitar and amplifier. I rode a Greyhound Bus from Mobile to Waycross.

Pee Wee King was born to a working-class, Polish/German family near Abrams, Wisconsin. He was christened Julius Frank Anthony Kuczynski and grew up playing polkas on the accordion. He formed his first band in high school. Gene Autry hired him as a back-up band at WLS Radio in Chicago and gave him the name "Pee Wee." Then Pee Wee, himself, changed his last name to King, in honor of Wayne King, the Waltz King. When Pee Wee formed his band he called them the Golden West Cowboys. The idea for the name came from a WLS trio, the Girls of The Golden West. Pee Wee and his band worked at WNOX Radio in Knoxville and at WHAS Radio in Louisville before moving to the WSM Grand Ole Opry in Nashville on June 26, 1937. They became the new hot band on the Opry, bringing with them the sounds of Western Swing. They were the most flamboyant and sophisticated of the bands hired on the Opry at that time.

They had six members. Pee Wee played the accordion. Milton Estes played guitar and banjo. The fiddler was Abner Sims. Comedy and bass was handled by Curley Rhodes. Curley's sister, Texas Daisy, yodeled and sang cowboy songs. Cowboy Jack Skaggs did a lot of the singing.

This band was organized. They introduced "play-on music" and "chasers" to the Opry. They also dressed fit to kill. They were polished, rehearsed, and read music—highly unusual in that day and time among hillbillies. They were among the first Opry musicians to join the Musicians' Union. The Opry was not unionized until it was learned that the Golden West Cowboys belonged to the Louisville chapter of the American Federation of Musicians. Local 257, Nashville, was well established but only welcomed classical performers. Their opinion was that country musicians were not professionals as they didn't read music. King convinced them that they were professionals and all his band members read music. After that, other Opry musicians joined the Nashville local and in a few years the Opry became unionized.

At the Opry for Royal Crown Cola. *From the left:* Don Davis, Shorty Reed, Chuck Wiggins, Becky Barfield, Pee Wee King, Jimmy Wilson, Buddy Herrell.

Pee Wee was also the first to bring his own booking agency with him. His wife was the daughter of J. L. Frank, who was an innovative promoter and booker. He had good contacts on the music scene. He was managing Gene Autry when he took over management of Pee Wee. This was about the time that Autry moved to Hollywood for a movie career.

When I got off that bus in Waycross, I had no time to get rested. I went to work immediately. This was a rare thing for a picker to be hired before they hit the city limits of Nashville.

The first order of the day was a rehearsal at a radio station. Radio stations are always on the second floor. No elevators in those small towns! Steel guitars and amps were heavy, even back then. Later, when I got to a double-neck, then a triple neck, man, you're talking heavy. You think a fiddle player is going to help you? No way! They make the same money as you do. We rehearsed at the station and learned all the tunes. I did fine. We played a 15-minute program to promote the show that night.

Oscar Davis, the promoter, was working with Frank, Pee Wee's manager. Oscar was one hell of a show promoter. He was flamboyant, dressing in silk suits with a gold chain across his vest and he wore big diamond rings. (When times got bad, he'd hock those rings, but times always got good again and he'd redeem them.) He would take over the microphone, get up on his tiptoes, and bark into it, "Come out and see Pee Wee King and his Golden West Cowboys tonight at a spectacular Opry show." We would begin playing and Becky Barfield would sing "Pair Of Broken Hearts." I took the introduction and played it perfectly. All went well.

But, that night at the show, when I was out there on stage, it suddenly dawned on me that I had never seen that many people before in my life as were in that auditorium. All those bright lights! I'd gone from a tent show to this. I was out there with my foot pedal and a guitar strap around my neck with my single neck steel in front of me.

Then Oscar said, "And now, here he is, from Mobile, Alabama—Don Davis with "Steel Guitar Rag!'" I got to shaking and my right foot on that volume control set up a vibrating sound. It was like I had St. Vitus Dance. Afterwards, the band said, "We never heard 'Steel Guitar Rag' played like that. Don't know how you did it, but keep doing it." The band members thought I was nothing less than great. They didn't know that vibrating sound came about because my foot was shaking on the pedal. Later that evening at the hotel, that clean underwear I brought came in handy. The next time I played and had calmed down, all I heard was, "Hey, man, how 'bout the vibrato?"

When I started with Pee Wee, our band members were me on steel, Jimmy Wilson on bass, Chuck Wiggins on rhythm guitar, Buddy Harrell on piano, and Becky Barfield, singer. Pee Wee played accordion. Hal Smith played fiddle. This was the first time I had seen Hal since he was billed as the "Fiddlin' Fool from Fiddlersville" when he was with Tex Dunn in Mobile.

When I went to work with Pee Wee, Minnie Pearl was part of the act. She decided to give me some motherly advice since I was so young. She told me that all those women who came backstage after the show all had diseases. She made me so afraid of them, I wouldn't even shake hands. (Later on I got over that problem.) I was like that dumb kid, Eb, on the *Green Acres* show. I was just dumb, green, and sixteen years old.

Back row: Buddy Harrell, Shorty Boyd, Jimmy Wilson, Don Davis, Bill Carr, Chuck Wiggins. **Front row:** Minnie Pearl, Doug Autry, unknown, Pee Wee King, Becky Barfield.

From left: Chuck Wiggins, Buddy Harrell, a promoter, Don Davis, Minnie Pearl, Pee Wee King riding the horse Boots, Becky Barfield, Jimmy Wilson, Doug Autry, Shorty Boyd, Bill Carr, horse trainer. *Photo courtesy of the Billy Robinson collection*.

The band at The Blue Room in Houston, Texas. **From left, back row:** Harold Bradley (guitar), Ferris Coursey (drums), Jimmy Wilson (bass), Buddy Harrall (piano). **Front row:** Don Davis (steel), Red Stewart (guitar), Shorty Boyd (fiddle), Pee Wee King (accordion). *Photo courtesy of the Harold Bradley collection.*

Becky Barfield singing, Pee Wee King (accordion), Don Davis (guitar).

Frankie "Pee Wee" King with San Antonio Rose and his Golden West Cowboys, 1946. **Standing, from left:** Chuck Wiggins, Don Davis, Jimmy Wilson, Pee Wee King, San Antonio Rose, Cowboy Copas. Kneeling: Redd Stewart, Shorty Boyd.

Northside Coliseum, Fort Worth, Texas, 1946. **Back row:** Buddy Harrell, Chuck Wiggins, Shorty Boyd, someone hidden, Don Davis. **Front row:** Pee Wee King, Minnie Pearl, unknown presenter.

Minnie Pearl. Photo inscribed, "To D-Donald—with happy memories of happy years on the road together—my best + most loving wishes, Minnie Pearl."

Minnie Pearl's birthday party at Northside Coliseum, Fort Worth, Texas, 1946.
To the right of the cake: Don Davis, Minnie Pearl, Pee Wee King.

One night, this lady came up to me backstage and slipped her hotel key in my hand and walked out the door. I chased her out the door yelling, "Ma'am, you forgot your key." I was so dumb I thought she had forgotten it while getting autographs. She ran like a scalded dog when she thought I was chasing her. Minnie saw it all, and, boy, did she laugh. Then, whenever she had an audience, she glorified in telling that story. I got so I'd beat her to the punch and tell it myself.

When we got into Nashville to work the Opry on Saturday night, I went right up to the Clarkston Hotel where I was to room with Buddy Harrell, the piano player. The room didn't have a bathroom, but it had a wash basin. You had to piss in the sink. The shower and commode were down the hall. The Clarkston had a coffee shop and all the hillbillies hung out there, drinking coffee or beer. That's when I first saw all those hillbilly musicians. You could tell 'em. They all had sideburns and wore plaid shirts. In those days, if you walked out on the street with your cowboy hat on, some bystander would say, "Hey, cowboy, where's your horse!" Now they don't do that. Nashville got used to us.

I went to work for Pee Wee and became a Golden West Cowboy the week before my Opry debut. It was the summer of 1945. I was 16 years old. When the big Saturday night arrived, I walked out on stage with them. I thought, "Hell, I am one of those Golden West Cowboys!" I looked out at the fans on that hot summer night and I realized this was the thrill of my life. I was going to play a solo on the Royal Crown Cola portion of the Grand Ole Opry. Not only that, the steel player had a big part in the theme song. The band would sing:

Turkey in the straw, turkey in the hay
Drink a Royal Crown Cola every single day.

Then the steel would go: *"Ooh-ah-h-h-h-!"* right up the whole neck.

That was a thrill. I'd been hearing other steel players doing that and I'd think, "If only I could do that!" Now I was. I don't know what was the bigger thrill, playing that glissando or playing my first solo, "Steel Guitar Rag."

I knew that everybody in Mobile was listening. I had told my cousins I was going to play and they spread the news. They talk about that night, even today: "The night Don played at the Grand Ole Opry." There were a lot more listeners in Alabama then than now. The Grand Ole Opry was the Saturday-night-happening then.

I remember that a cooler of R.C. Cola was brought out on stage and musicians and stage hands would gather around and drink those cold RCs and watch those poor people in the audience at the old Ryman Auditorium sweating and moving those fans back and forth. No air conditioning! They had paid the whopping sum of 65 cents to get in.

Yes, I felt I was a seasoned performer, but that one night my throat was dry and the hand that was holding my bar trembled ever so slightly. But my foot was steady on the pedal and this 16-year-old passed the test with flying colors for all my friends and neighbors. "Take it away, boys," as the Solemn Old Judge used to say.

I was in Heaven from that time on. Pee Wee paid me $45 a week. This included my performance at the Opry, as I was paid weekly. We traveled in a 1939 Ford stretch limo. A 1940 panel truck followed with our instruments and luggage. We did as many as five shows a day at theaters and concert dates, staying on the road night and day. Meanwhile we had to be back at our mandatory Saturday night Opry show.

I was always glad to be back at the Opry. My heroes were all there. Roy Acuff was one. I noticed he always wore hand-painted ties. When Pee Wee played El Paso, Texas, I went over to Mexico and I saw these hand-painted ties. I saw one that had a bullfighter on it. It almost glowed in the dark. It looked like one of those Elvis-on-Velvet pictures you see today. I thought one of them was beautiful and, man, how I loved Roy Acuff. So I bought it for seventy-five cents and brought it back with me and gave it to Roy. I had only been at the Opry a short time and I wanted to impress him. Oswald and Roy's band doubled over laughing, but Roy actually wore that tie the next Saturday night. "Don't disappoint the kid," you know. I didn't know it at the time, but, boy, was that tie ugly!

Roy Acuff with a
hand-painted necktie.

My other hero was Eddy Arnold. He wore real elegant, expensive sport shirts. He wore a T-shirt under them, but in those days, you didn't wear a T-shirt that showed at the neck. I noticed in the dressing room that he would take scissors and cut the neck in a V and fold it down. I went to some little town in Alabama with Pee Wee, and saw in a store downtown some V-neck T-shirts. They were new, just come out. I bought a whole package for about seventy-five cents. The only problem was, they only had one size: small. I bought them and gave them to Eddy the next Saturday night. He put one on right then and there. Man, it looked like a girl's halter top! The guys in the dressing room tried hard not to laugh. Eddy was a big man. He was so gracious. He said, "Thank you, Don." And he wore it that night. He probably threw them away after that. I may not have impressed Eddy and Roy, but they sure impressed me.

We played two shows on Saturday nights at the Opry, one early show before 9:00 PM and one late show after 9:00 PM. We did anything to relieve the boredom between shows. One night, the guitar player Ray Edenton and I were sitting on a bench on the back side of the curtains waiting for our spot to play. It was the Saturday night before Easter and Hank Snow was singing "Easter Parade." Now Hank had his way of pronouncing words, with a Canadian accent. The word parade became "paah-rade." Of course we didn't plan it, but we decided to sing with Hank. Every time he'd come to a line that had parade in it, like "You'll be the grandest lady in the Easter Parade," Ray and I would make a trio out of it, singing "Easter Paah-rade," in harmony with Hank, pronouncing it just like him. Hank kept right on singing and so did we. We had a real trio going. Sleepy McDaniel and Chubby Wise, who worked for Hank, went almost white, they were so afraid. You see, Hank was one of those perfectionists who allowed no deviation from his planned program. But after he got off stage and passed us, all Hank said in passing was, "Mighty good job. We'll have to do it again sometime." We never knew if he knew we were imitating him singing "paah-rade" or if he didn't really know.

We didn't make much money, but we all had a lot of fun. One time, a bunch of us were having a little drink outside the dressing room while our friend, Howard White, steel player with Cowboy Copas, was entertaining us. Howard was a back-stage comedian. I think one of his best acts was an impersonation of Roy Acuff. He had Roy down pat, his mannerisms, his speech, and he sounded just like him. He had a routine he made up having to do with Dunbar Cave and Brother Oswald getting thrown off a horse. (Roy owned Dunbar Cave, a resort, then.) It was a comical act. Howard was doing his thing, when Roy Acuff, himself, walked up behind Howard and stood there. We didn't let on that Roy was back there and it just made us laugh harder. Howard was really on a roll, really getting down with it. When he finished his act, Roy said, "That's the best I ever heard." We all cracked up. Roy was laughing and Howard took off. Roy later told Howard, "You can do this act all you want to, but I've already made all the money out of it."

On Saturday nights at the Opry, we usually added a novelty song. One such song was a little ditty called "Uncle Noah's Ark." It was a trio-type song and I believe that Pee Wee, Chuck Wiggens, and Jimmy Wilson made up this singing trio. It went like this:

The duck went quack, the cow went moo
The rooster went cock-a-doodle-doo
All were there on Uncle Noah's Ark.
There were horses and cattle and fowl of the air

Even the long-eared jack-ass was there
All were there on Uncle Noah's Ark.

The only problem we had with that song was when we performed it at the Opry, the head honcho, George D. Hay, known as the Solemn Old Judge, sorta censored everything, even some of the picking. If Slim Idaho and I got a little wild with our picking, he'd admonish us and cool us down. When the trio sang "Uncle Noah's Ark," they had to substitute the word "jassack" for "jackass," singing "even the long-eared jassack was there."

Well, on one particular Saturday night, the trio was singing and Jimmy Wilson, playing bass, leaned into the microphone to sing his part about the "jassack." In those days there was only one microphone and when it was your time to sing, you leaned in closer to the microphone. Jimmy leaned in to sing his lines. He sang:

There were horses and cattle and fowl of the air
Even the long ass jack ear was there.

He came out louder than the rest of the trio, and "the long ass jack ear" came out clear as a bell on that clear-channel, 50,000-watt station. Opry performances were live and there was no taking it back. The Solemn Old Judge was more than solemn after that performance. The rest of us couldn't stop laughing.

WSM created a show for Friday nights they called the "Friday Night Frolics." We simply called it the "Frolics." It was held in Studio C in the old National Life Building on the fifth floor. At first there was no charge for the show. (That show is now called the "Friday Night Opry.") We all played the "Frolics."

Chet Atkins, a guitar player at the Opry then, played that show too. Now there are two things that Chet could not stand: the "Frolics" and the least bit of electrical shock. He would come unglued at the least bit of electricity. We used to have ground switches on our amplifiers. So, one night at the "Frolics," I was standing close to Chet's amp and I reversed the ground switches on his amp. He touched that ground wire and he hollered, "Shit!" The mike was live and his voice went out over those 50,000 watts. Then he turned to me and said, "Damn you!" Just a normal night on radio!

I knew Chet very well, and I knew he had this beautiful D'Angelico guitar. He was very shy and introverted in those days, just another guitar player. He was so proud of that guitar, treated it like it was Waterford Crystal. Now I knew a guy in Pennsylvania who also owned a D'Angelico, but he had been in a car wreck and his guitar was destroyed. All that was left was the neck. The body was in splinters, but you could still read D'Angelico on the neck. I bought it from him for $50. WSM had a daily show called "Noontime Neighbors." Chet and I were both booked on the show. I got there first and waited for Chet to come in. When Chet came in, he set his guitar case down and went to the bathroom. When he left. I went and got the gunny sack in which I had put the busted guitar. I took Chet's guitar out of its case and put in the busted one. Chet came back, opened his guitar case, looked at that busted guitar, sat down in a chair, and turned white as a sheet. The blood just left his face. Then I walked in, carrying his D'Angelico and handed it to him. All he said was, "Thanks!" And that's all he ever said about that incident. Chet Atkins and I remained friends throughout the years.

In 1945 and '46, before Pee Wee organized his big cowboy band, we did mostly western songs like "Tumbling Tumbleweeds." Becky Barfield was our yodeler. If you did a concert north of the Mason-Dixon Line without a yodeler, you risked being tarred and feathered.

We were working at the Keel Auditorium in St. Louis, a really big auditorium. Little Becky Barfield was with us, of course. One of her songs was called "Chime Bells." The stage was a long one. The way we always brought her on was to play her introduction and then vamp until she was ready and got to the mike. There were all these extra bright foot lights on, blinding us and Becky. Pee Wee's high school horse had just been put through all his paces and the horse had left his "signature" in the middle of the stage. Then it was time for Little Becky Barfield to do her act. We started playing, and she came skipping out with this great big jumbo guitar, bigger than she was. Her little boots hit that horse manure and she did a back flip, bam! right down in the middle of that stage. She busted that guitar all to hell and had horse manure hanging off the fringe of her little outfit. Of course, the poor girl left the stage and went into seclusion in the bathroom, even locking the door. She "chimed that bell" that night, all right. (Little Becky Barfield finally went to California and worked with Spade Cooley, the great western swing band leader. She married Cameron Hill, a guitar player with Cooley, and Bob Wills.)

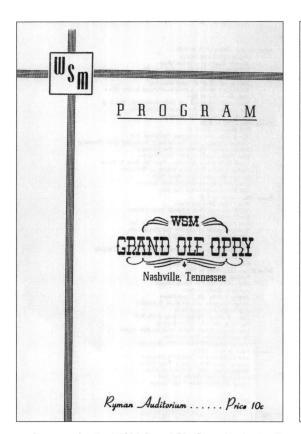

Program for the WSM Grand Ole Opry, Nashville, Tennessee, Ryman Auditorium, Saturday, May 21, 7:30 to 12 P.M. Don Davis played in the band from 9:30 to 10 P.M., and the featured song "Bye-Bye Blues."

We began our nationwide tour in Tampa, Florida. We stayed at the high-class Tampa Terrace Hotel. It was there that a guy who worked for J. L. Frank suggested that I needed a suit. He took me to a chain clothier known as "Steins" and bought me a suit for $27.50. This guy's name was Tom Parker, yes, the same Col. Tom Parker who later became known as Elvis Presley's manager. At the time he was known as "Wabbet," as in the cartoon character, Bugs Bunny. Parker's claim to fame then was his impersonation of Smiley Burnette, Gene Autry's sidekick, and Bugs Bunny. I have heard stories about Col. Tom being tight with money. However, he never asked me for the $27.50 back for the Stein suit.

Getting to show dates was not easy in the 1940s, as rationing had not yet been lifted on gasoline. The law was that holders of "A" cards, the most common, were limited to four gallons a week. If you could show hardship you might get a "B" card, which granted 150 miles a month to get to work. Some few got "C" cards that were reserved for vital war jobs and got 470 monthly miles. With the cards, coupons looking like stamps were issued. Pee Wee and J. L. Frank were creative. They knew that farmers were allowed special allotments for gas for farm machines like tractors to keep the food supply ample. They always had a surplus, and Pee Wee and Frank knew enough farmers where they could get a lot of gas. Another strategy was to cut a deal with the Department of Defense where they traded entertainment at an Army, Navy, or Marine base for tires and gas. To be thrifty, re-cap tires were bought, and there was a thriving black market industry that could be tapped. With creative ideas like these, Pee Wee and other acts were able to keep working and make their tours.

I was fascinated with big Western Swing Bands and Pee Wee listened to me talk constantly about Bob Wills and Spade Cooley. Western Swing is a combination of traditional country fiddles and big band swing, perfect for dancing. In the southeast, dances were held in barns with a typical string line-up: banjo, guitar, and fiddle. In the southwest, dance halls became the equivalent of barn dances. Bob Wills rose to prominence in Texas with his Texas Playboys in the mid-1930s, rivaling the big bands of the swing era, like Tommy Dorsey. Wills used basic fiddles, drums, piano, and steel guitar, but he also added horns. He felt the more horns he used, the classier the band would be. The term, "Western Swing" came into use after World War II. Bands then became sleeker and faster. Bob Wills and the Texas Playboys then began working dance halls exclusively. He had a string of hits, among them "San Antonio Rose." Spade Cooley, based in California, was smoother and classier than Wills. He has been called the Lawrence Welk of Western Swing. He played the big ballrooms in Hollywood and had two of the most famous steel players, Noel Boggs and Joaquin Murphy.

All of us Golden West Cowboys got excited about Western Swing. We thought that it was the "thing." So, after listening to us, Pee Wee decided he wanted to do a dance tour in Texas. In order to secure the dates he had to beef-up the band with drums and electric guitars. He hired Farris Coursey, who was the staff drummer for Owen Bradley's WSM Orchestra. Farris used vacation time to go on tour with us. Pee Wee also hired Harold Bradley, who later became one of the pioneers of the Nashville Sound. Pee Wee then hired a permanent drummer, Sticks McDonald, who had played with Bob Wills and Spade Cooley, and our band built from there. Pee Wee borrowed some of the Bob Wills sound, and smoothness and class from Spade Cooley, and we started playing dance halls in Texas and Oklahoma that were so big you almost had to use binoculars to see the bandstand. There would be 2000 people on the dance floor at one time. Sometimes the men danced with beer bottles in their back pockets. Everybody danced; women even danced with each other. There was a war on and a shortage of men. We played dance songs, sad songs, novelties, and love songs in a variety of styles and tempos. Pee Wee said he wanted to make people feel good and want to dance.

Now, with Pee Wee's big band, I needed to get a more powerful amplifier and a more sophisticated steel guitar. I had become friends with Noel Boggs, Bob Wills's steel player at that time. Noel had just made a deal with Leo Fender to use Fender's new double-neck guitar. So Noel agreed to sell me his Epiphone, two-neck "Electar," which had eight strings on one neck and seven on the other, a monstrous hexagon-shaped thing. I tuned the eight string neck to A6 and the seven string neck to C6. I really enjoyed playing this guitar. It was my first bonafied, manufactured, double-neck steel guitar and the first guitar I had with an eight-string neck. I even had a stand built for it to keep it off my lap.

The Plantation Club, Nashville. **Front center:** Danny Dill. **Left to right:** Curly Rhodes, Mary Claire Rhodes, Annie Lou Dill, Cousin Jody's wife, Betty Jo McCord, Dale Potter, Billy Robinson, Jimmy Self, Don Davis, Billy Stewart. *Photo courtesy of the Billy Robinson collection.*

Pee Wee was playing in a place at Houston that had two dance halls, one downstairs and one upstairs. Bob Wills would play upstairs for a set and we would play downstairs. Then we would swap places. Noel Boggs, Wills's steel player, talked Wills and Pee Wee into letting him and me stay put while the rest of the band traded places. Boggs assured Wills that I could play his music. I could play every note exactly like Boggs. I had his style down pat. So that's how I got to sit in with Bob Wills. I'm the only musician that Bob Wills ever allowed to sit in with his band.

The guitar I bought from Noel Boggs did just fine. I really liked to play it. I recorded with it when we went to Chicago in 1946 to record for RCA Victor, with A&R Director Steve Sholes. I made scale, which was $25 per session. (Later the Union raised the scale to $41.25.) We recorded "Steel Guitar Rag." Pee Wee hired Harold Bradley to play guitar and included a vocal by Tommy Sosebee. The music had been written earlier by Leon McAuliffe and the lyrics were by Merle Travis and Cliff Stone. On that session we also recorded "Tennessee Central No. 9" and "Texas Toni Lee," both written by Fred Rose. The band also recorded a sing-along on "Southland Polka," an original by Pee Wee and Redd Stewart. The first release off that session was "Steel Guitar Rag," backed with "Tennessee Central No. 9."

While I was doing that session, Cliff Carlisle dropped by the studio before his scheduled session, following us. He asked me to play dobro on his session. Cliff was a great dobro player, however, he was singing on his session and he thought it would be better to have another dobro player. I had never played dobro before, but I felt like I could. A dobro is a six-string acoustical instrument, played like an electric steel guitar with picks and bar. So in December 1946, I played dobro while Cliff Carlisle sang. It was an honor, as Cliff was a pioneer in our business. In the 1920s, Cliff and a partner, Wilbur Ball, became the first blue-yodeling duet. Among country pickers, Cliff was the first to use the resonator dobro guitar, made by the Dopyera Brothers in Los Angeles. Cliff and his brother Bill recorded and performed together for decades. Their "Rainbow At Midnight" became a Top-10 record for King Records. By 1947, Cliff still recorded but he quit playing shows.

I left Chicago with some of the band members to go to Cincinnati to record with a new member of our group, Cowboy Copas. Copas became a recording star for King Records with hits "Filipino Baby" and "Tragic Romance." We were all set to record with Copas, under the direction of Syd Nathan, who owned King. Then I discovered I had a problem with this guitar I had learned to depend on. I found out the pick-ups had failed and were producing only a faint sound from the strings. A quick-thinking engineer on Syd's staff rigged up a makeshift pre-amp. We went on with the session. Much to my embarrassment, when the hit "Signed, Sealed and Delivered" was released and I heard this recording on the radio, I could hear shrill, ear-piercing sounds of my picks touching the strings. I had no choice but to live with it. That is now history.

Syd Nathan had heard these strange sounds from my guitar, I guess, because sometime later at a session he told me he wanted me to do a drum sound. "On my steel?," I asked. "Yeah," he said, "Just go 'varoom chic chic, varoom chic chic'." Damn, I couldn't go "varoom chic chic" on a steel guitar. I guess after "Signed, Sealed and Delivered," he thought I could do any kind of a sound.

In 1946, I recorded with Cowboy Copas at King Records in Cincinnati. Also on that session were Jimmy Wilson, guitar, Redd Stewart and Shorty Boyd, fiddles, Chuck Wiggins, bass, and Pee Wee King, accordion. We recorded "No More Roamin," "Jukebox Blues," and "Sweet Thing." It was in 1947 that I recorded "Signed, Sealed and Delivered" with Copas. Hank Garland, guitar, Autry Inman, bass, and Fiddlin' Red Herron were on that session also.

I cooked up a scheme to "get" Cowboy Copas and Carl Smith. I knew that Copas and Carl were coming in from St. Louis on Eastern Air Lines. Now, this was in the early days at Berry Field, before the International Airport was even in the planning stages. The planes all arrived outside of the small terminal. There was a fence beside the runway so the gawkers could go outside, lean on the fence, and watch the DC-3s arrive. The terminal was just a small building some 200 feet away.

I drafted Don "Suds" Slayman, Ray Edenton, Lightning Chance, and Floyd "Mousie" Robinson into the act. I talked to a friend at Eastern and they agreed to let us set up a welcoming band for the dignitaries arriving. They set up a stage for us. (Ray Edenton remembers it was a four-wheel dolly.) We had amplifiers, microphones, and everything set up out there; we were there with all our instruments. We put up a big sign that said, "Welcome Home." It was cold and we all had our topcoats on. Well, the plane arrived and as they got off, we began playing "Filipino Baby." Carl Smith spotted us and took off the other way. Copas got off the plane grinning from ear to ear while we played his hit song. (We sounded terrible!) After all the hoopla was over, a bystander asked me, "Who was that guy in the ten gallon hat?" "Oh," I said, "That was Cowboy Copas!" "Cowboy WHO?," he asked.

For a short period of time, Joe Frank brought in a star-studded cast of performers: Minnie Pearl, Cowboy Copas, Doug Autry (Gene's brother), and Grandpa Jones—adding to our troupe of a ten-piece band. Also added were two horses, a trainer, and a caravan of vehicles to haul all the people and animals. The only thing we lacked to compete with Barnum & Bailey were elephants and lions. What a sight we made on the highways! As we passed people waved and blew their horns at us.

The spring of the year after I became a Golden West Cowboy, Pee Wee announced we were about to embark on a big tent show. It alarmed me, as I had flashbacks about the tent shows I worked with Charley Sailors, tents with just side walls and seats of concrete blocks and two-by-sixes. I started thinking, "Oh, my God, back to the tent again, back where I started!" However, Frank was quite a promoter. He was experienced and knew what he was doing. He struck a deal with Barnum and Bailey

Don Davis with a steel guitar made by Jimmy Wyndam from North Carolina.

and leased one of their huge circus tents. Lo and behold, that was a marvel. Instead of setting it up on a vacant lot, it was set up on a piece of property the size of a farm. He figured out central locations where we could draw people from several towns. People came to our show in droves from everywhere and filled that gigantic tent up. A professional crew put up and took down the tent. A big portable generator furnished electricity. It was an extravaganza! It all had to be transported from venue to venue. The crew had their own cook tent with a chef.

My friend, guitar player Grady Martin, and I were both in our teens, great big overgrown boys. We decided that somehow we had to work our way into that cook tent and get some of that good food those boys were having. When we got into a new town, we volunteered to help those roustabouts set that tent up. After that, Grady and I were allowed to eat with the guys at the cook tent. All we had to do was work a little to get that good food.

We had quite a package show. Added to Pee Wee King and the Golden West Cowboys were Curly Fox, a Tennessee trick fiddler, and Texas Ruby, both Opry regulars. Ruby had a robust voice, known as the "Sophie Tucker of the Cowgirl Singers."

Also on the show were Jamup and Honey, a mainstay of the Opry. Lee Davis "Honey" Wilds came to Nashville as a partner of Lee Roy "Lasses" White in 1932. They had been part of the "All Stars Minstrel Show." They had their own minstrel show on WSM on Friday nights. WSM publicity referred to White as the "Dean of the burnt cork artists." They appeared on the Opry in April 1934 as "Lasses and Honey."

Hank Snow and Howard White, steel guitar player and jokester, backstage at the Grand Ole Opry.

JAMUP and HONEY
STARS OF
W S M GRAND OLE OPRY

Jamup and Honey, blackface stars of WSM, at the Grand Ole Opry.

As they were now appearing in front of more modern audiences, they changed their act to adapt to a newer format. They still appeared in blackface, tuxedos, and white gloves and became very popular, getting high touring fees, recording on Bluebird Records, and issuing annual song books and jokes. The minstrel show is one of the few purely American forms of entertainment. It was kind of a vaudeville show in which performers blackened their faces with burnt cork. They sat in a semi-circle on stage and an interlocutor acted as a "Straight Man." The shows, also performed on showboats, featured comedy routines, songs, variety acts, and dancing. The Christy Minstrels and the All-Star Minstrels were famous troupes that played the Orpheum Theater in Nashville. By 1936, Lasses White moved to Hollywood. Honey Wilds continued on in the minstrel tradition with different partners he called "Jamup" (Tom Woods, Bunny Biggs, and Harry LeVan). They were the last of the minstrel show acts on the Opry when times changed.

Grady and I, the pranksters of the troupe, heard that the roustabouts had killed a big king snake about five feet long when they were clearing an area for the tent. We decided we could use that snake to pull a gag on an unsuspecting act. We got a string and tied it around the snake's neck and put it on one side of the stage. Then we pulled the string to the other side of the stage so we could drag that sucker across the stage. We waited until the opportune moment. Jamup and Honey happened to be doing their act, and when they were in the middle of their routine we started pulling the string with that snake across the stage. As we pulled the snake right in front of them, they looked down and the excitement began right then. Honey made an exit; I don't know if he went to the right or left or front of the stage. He just disappeared, leaving Jamup out there to finish their act. Harry LeVan was playing Jamup at the time. He backed up away from the snake and, being the pro that he was, continued his act. I don't remember how long it took us to find Honey.

Uncle Dave Macon was also a star of this tent show extravaganza. Uncle Dave was known as the "Dixie Dewdrop" on the Opry. He carried three banjos, each tuned differently, and according to Judge Hay, "He could whip a banjo until it cried." He was also known for making his own "sippin' whiskey." He used to take it along with him on the road in a little jug. We all understood that none of us were gonna get a taste of that sippin' whiskey. Uncle Dave didn't share his private stock. No way!

Uncle Dave traveled with Curly Fox and Texas Ruby in an old Cadillac limo. Uncle Dave rode in the back. I told Curly I bet I could get a drink outta that jug, and he bet me five dollars I couldn't. He said, "There's no way you'll get a drink out of that jug no matter how much Dave likes you. He just won't give you a drink from his private stock."

I figured I could find a way to do it. Back then it was about impossible to get Jack Daniel's, but I managed to get a half-pint from Whitey Ford, the Duke of Paducah. (Ken "Loosh" Marvin called a half-pint an e-flat.) I talked Curly into letting me ride with them. I got in the back seat with Uncle Dave; we had become good friends. I had laid plans for getting a drink of Dave's sippin' whiskey. Curly was watching me in the rear view mirror. I pulled out my half-pint of Jack Daniel's and held it in my hand so Uncle Dave could eye-ball it. I figured if he got to looking at it, he would want a taste of it. Finally I opened it up and offered him a taste; so he took it and then I tasted it a little. Curly was still watching us as we passed that Jack Daniel's back and forth. Then I said, "You know, Uncle Dave, I have never had any homemade whiskey. I'd like to have a little taste of it, not a lot, just a little taste." Dave reached over and got his jug, since I had been so nice sharing that Jack Daniel's with him. He handed me the jug and I held it up high where Curly could see me. I took a taste, handed the jug back to Uncle Dave and held up five fingers for Curly to see, to remind him he owed me five dollars.

After a short period into all this extravaganza, I suggested we add more flair to the band by jumping up at the end of each tune and hitting a final chord. This idea really caught on, so we added more jumping. One time, one of the band members was standing on the cord to Redd Stewart's fiddle pick-up and did not jump in time. When Redd jumped, he left his fiddle behind. It got to the point where you had to be about an acrobat to be a member of the band.

With the big band, we had to have arrangements, so I was elected for the job. Pee Wee played the accordion—not just any accordion, it was expensive. It had oboes, fiddles, every sound you can imagine on it. Now, I don't like accordions, so I put his part in as a fiddle or some other instrument. It took him quite a while to figure out what I was doing.

Our whole band was dressed classy. These were the days before Nudie made all those Western clothes. The Opry bands were still wearing bib overalls and checked shirts. Our outfits were made by Turk, the rodeo tailor. He made costumes for stars like Gene Autry and Tex Ritter. We really stood out; we were flashy. I don't know what happened to my gold nylon shirt. Now my shirts were satin.

There comes a time when any musician gets tired of traveling and Pee Wee was no exception. He decided he was going to move to Louisville and just play music around there. When Pee Wee announced he was leaving, I decided it was time to move on, too. I had been a Golden West Cowboy for about three years.

Roy Ayres replaced me. According to Ayres, "I received an unexpected note from Pee Wee. He said Don had left the band and had gone to the West Coast and would I sit-in with the band. Earlier I had written to Don, care of Pee Wee King at WSM, to ask Don about a National guitar. Don never received my letter, but Pee Wee opened the mail and in that way knew I was a steel player and my name and address." So in that way, Pee Wee King's Golden West Cowboys carried on with Roy Ayres, their new steel player. Time marches on.

Chapter 5
A Grand Ole Lady

There is a house at 620 Boscobel Street in East Nashville—a yellow stone house between Shelby Avenue and Woodland Street. It became famous because of the Grand Ole Opry stars and musicians it housed. Delia Upchurch was the owner and "Den Mother" to all of us. We called her "Mom." Mom (or "Ma" as some would say) was just a Nashville homemaker who opened her house in East Nashville to struggling young musicians, many of whom were so young they were experiencing their first time away from their own home and family.

Shorty Boyd was the first person who stayed there at a time when Mom's husband, Louis K. Upchurch, was still alive. Shorty talked them into letting me stay there, too, as we were both members of Pee Wee King's band then. When Mr. Upchurch died, I was in California, and when I got back Mom was grieving.

I talked Mom into letting other musicians live there, because I knew if anybody could cheer her up it would be a bunch of dang hillbilly pickers. I told her it would be an income she needed. When she agreed, everybody started moving in there.

Her good cooking, and especially her rates, attracted all the pickers. We only paid $7 a week for board and she charged 85 cents for dinner and 75 cents for breakfast. There were three bedrooms downstairs and two upstairs. There was one shared bath and, wonder of all wonders, there wasn't much arguing over its use. Think of a dozen hillbillies all getting ready to play the Opry at the same time on a Saturday night. We had the run of the house, using the living room as our own.

She had one phone, only one line and no call-waiting. Mail was neatly stacked in the downstairs hall.

The hopefuls were coming into town with no money, no jobs, and no friends, each of them with the same dream of getting on the Opry. They needed a home and somebody to look after them until they got started. Mom was just the person to do that for them.

One thing that Mom didn't allow in her house was any form of alcohol. She was an avid church-goer and a Democrat. You could find her every Sunday at Eastview Church of Christ on Shelby Street. Howard White (Morgan called him Sylvester), steel player, was one of Mom's longest residents at 10 years. Once he made a tour in Canada and came home with a recipe for Peach Brandy. He managed to make it in Mom's basement without her knowledge. It had to ferment for 30 days and before the time was up, Mom found it. She made him pour it out. "Honey," she said, "those Revenuers might come in and close this place down."

Then another time, someone gave Howard a gallon of moonshine. He brought it home to Mom's and hid it in the closet. As he was leaving to go on tour with Cowboy Copas, he let Ray Edenton, a guitar player also living at Mom's, have a taste. While

Howard was gone, Edenton took that 'shine over to some girl's house across the street and had a party. Ten days later, when Howard came back, he looked for his moonshine and found the jug almost empty. Edenton said, "There was a lot of hell raised." But as Howard said, "Not enough to attract Mom's attention."

"Well," Mom used to say, "My boys don't drink too much, but they always want a lot of water early in the morning." Mom used to take a sip of Mogen David Wine (she called it David Morgan Wine), and every once in a while she chewed a little tobacco. Mom used to put up with a lot from us, but she loved it. She always knew when each of us came in. After all, we were her boys.

One night, Dale Potter and I came in after midnight after playing the Opry. We went back to Mom's bedroom, pulled her covers back and jumped into bed with her. As we ran for our own rooms, Mom was still shouting, "You boys! I don't know what I'm going to do with you."

Don Davis and "Mom" Upchurch, 1940s.

We aggravated her all the time. That's probably what kept her going. She loved us and we loved her. By the time I went into the Army, I was like her son. So much so that when Faron Young wanted to rent my room from her while I was gone, Mom warned him up front, "That's Don's room and when he comes back, you're out." Faron said, "Well, look, if I talk to him, maybe we could room together." Mom said, "That's up to him."

Once Dale Potter and I bought a motorcycle from Grady Martin. It was a nice big Harley 74 with a big seat on it. Mom kept telling us, "You're gonna get killed on that thing one day." Then one day when it was in the back yard, Dale coaxed her into sitting on it just to see how comfortable it was. While she was remarking that it really was comfortable after all, Dale jumped on the cycle, kicked it, and took off. Wow, what a ride!

Grady Martin, the finest guitar player in Nashville, and I spent a lot of time together when we both lived at Mom's. At this time, Grady's wife had left him and he was in a foul mood most of the time. He'd go out looking for trouble and, of course, if I was with him there were two of us looking for trouble. Usually the evening would end in a fight somewhere. Now, there was this place called the Glenview Inn where a lot of us drank beer, put nickels in the Seeburg 100 Selector Jukebox and shot pool. It was right off the East Nashville side of the old Shelby Bridge on South First Street. Mr. Fleming, the owner, ran a real straight dive. Grady and I were in a bunch of fights there. Then one day, somebody from "The Glenview," as we called it, called Grady at Mom's and told him that he would not be admitted to the Glenview anymore and to tell Don Davis he was barred too. Well, Grady didn't tell me. He waited until we were riding by one day and he pulled into the parking lot and asked me to go into the Glenview and get him a package of cigarettes. Being perfectly innocent to the fact that I was barred from there, I went in. They promptly threw me out saying I was never to come in there again. Grady thought that was the funniest thing he'd ever seen—me getting thrown out of the Glenview on my butt. What a laugh! Mr. Fleming didn't kid. He kept a big, hog-leg pistol right by the cash register. The Glenview taught me two things: (1) Beer bottles, in those days, don't break and (2) pay no attention to people who say, "Look-out for the little guys." It's these big dudes that weigh in at 280 pounds who are dangerous.

On any Saturday night after leaving Mom's, we would head for our Opry date. And of course, we had a lot of time on our hands between shows. That's when we would head for another "Mom's," a beer place that Louise "Mom" Hackler and her husband John had. The back door of this "Mom's" was off the alley, a little to the left of the Opry back stage entrance. We musicians drank beer there and swapped lies and listened to Ernest Tubb sing about lost love on the juke box. We were all one great big happy family. Mom catered to us, calling us her Opry boys. She had a shillelagh, an Irish club, and if one of us Opry boys came in and there wasn't a seat, she would ask the non-musician to get up and give her Opry boy that seat. If the person refused, she got her shillelagh after him. Now, Mom Hacker became curious about the other "Mom" across the river who ran the boarding house. One day, Buddy Emmons and I were sipping a cool one and Mom asked us, "Who is that woman across the river who calls herself "Mom?" We explained to her who Mom Upchurch was. Mom Hackler then turned to Buddy and I and said, "Well, I'm the original Mom, ain't that right Buddy!"

Tootsie Bess came along later and bought the old place and kept on catering to us. She wielded a long hat pin. The old tavern was run down, but there were pictures of all of us downstairs, and on the upstairs walls were autographs of the famous and not-so-famous. Tootsie renamed the old place "Tootsie's Orchid Lounge," although it was less of an Orchid Lounge than it was a watering hole. She painted the outside purple and the old place became famous, thanks to the show business people who hung-out there, wrote songs there, and fell in love there. And that's how Mom's place became an orchid lounge.

I went to Mom Hackler's a lot more after I got thrown out of the Glenview. Dale Potter and I spent a lot of time just having fun there. Any time any musicians were gathered together, there were always hangers-on who just wanted to be around us. Two of the most famous were Junior and Muscles. They had nothing to do with the music business but were just there to have fun. Junior was a big, six-foot-two man, probably weighing 220 pounds. He worked on a milk truck and had a speech problem. Muscles was maybe five-foot-two and weighed about 80 pounds. He sold newspapers and talked real fast. One night, Junior asked Dale Potter if he could loan him ten dollars; he promised to pay it back the next week. Muscles patted his leg and said, "That's right, Dale. If he don't, I will." Dale looked at me, grinned and said, "Now, that's security, ain't it!"

It was against the law to bring hard liquor into Mom's, but Junior kept a pint of whiskey in his back pocket. While Junior talked to us, Muscles would put his hand in Junior's back pocket, take out the bottle, unscrew the cap, take a long drink and then slip the bottle back in Junior's pocket. Junior never knew it and we didn't inform him. One night I saw Junior and I asked him what he had been doing. He said, "Got a job driving the bus for Lester and Earl," (Flatt and Scruggs). "Really," I said, "With Lester and Earl?" "Yup," he said. "Where y'all going?" I asked. "England!," he said. "You driving all the way to England?" I asked. Junior said, "You've got that god dang right!"

One night after Mom's became Tootsie's, I was sitting there with a table full of Opry boys, including one of our great steel players with his bride from Europe. She was sitting right beside me. I was my usual self, telling jokes and road stories. I noticed she was staring at me, listening with her elbow on the table and her chin in her hand. All at once, she blurted right out of the blue, with her cute foreign accent, "Huh! I bet you foch everybody you see!" Wow! I didn't know this girl, had never seen her before and I didn't know what to say. All the guys went crazy, pointing at me with a "Yeah, yeah!" If she meant to attract attention, she sure did.

The nice thing about Mom's boarding house was we always had a place to bed down after a night of smoke-filled bars. It didn't matter how many fights we had been in or how much we drank, there were always friends there.

The people who stayed at Mom's read like a *Who's Who of Country Music*. She kept us all: stars, musicians, songwriters, whatever. The only credential asked-for was that you be involved in Country Music. She loved her music Country style. Some of her roomers, besides Shorty Boyd and myself, were: Howard White, Ray Edenton, Grandpa Jones, the whole Carter Family, Dale Potter, Carl Smith, Joel Price, Faron Young, Gordon Terry, Lightnin' Chance, Harold Morrison, Walter Haynes, Shorty Lavender, George McCormick, Johnny Johnston, Buddy Spicher, Buddy Emmons, Grady Martin, Hank Garland, Donnie Young (Johnny Paycheck), Butterball Paige, Darrell McCall, Stonewall Jackson, Stan Hitchcock, Jimmy Elrod, Benny Williams, Lloyd Green, Hank Cochran, Joe Edwards and, as they say in show biz, "many others."

It became a status symbol to live at Mom's. Heck, it was home! There were always other musicians or writers hanging out there. The artists, bookers, and studios in town knew just where to call when they needed a musician. Somebody called every day to book somebody. And the girls! They knew where to find us, but we were not allowed any visitors in our rooms, a rule we all respected. We just didn't do that. Many a song was written there, many a song was plugged there, many a chord was learned there.

There have been other boarding houses for musicians, several on Music Row, but none of them were run by a good, Christian woman like Mom, with the integrity and innate knowledge of how to keep us happy but straight. When Delia "Mom" Upchurch turned 80, she quit renting rooms. She died in 1976 at age 85. Back then, there was not a home like hers and today there is no-one taking her place. She really was the Grand Ole Lady of Country Music.

A few days ago, I drove down Boscobel Street, stopping across the street from Number 620. An elderly lady was standing on the front steps. It could have been Mom. I got out and introduced myself. Her name is Alveda Newman. Mrs. Newman's son, a Nashville fireman, bought the house from the Upchurch family. Through the years she had learned a little about her home's history. I looked around. Mom's neatly trimmed yard was now overgrown with bushes and weeds, but our home-away-from-home is still standing, in all its glory. Neither rain, sleet, snow, or tornado has moved that old stone house one inch. It has survived! "Come and see me again," were Mrs. Newman's parting words. It could have been Mom's words, echoing through the years, as I left on tour.

From left: "Mom" Upchurch, Jean Stewart, Shorty Boyd, "Pop" Upchurch, Don Davis, 1940s.

Chapter 6

WEST COAST INTERLUDE

When Pee Wee announced he was leaving in 1947, Eddie Hill told me he was going to Memphis to start a show for WMPS Radio. He asked me to go with him. The Louvin Brothers, Ira and Charlie, were going also, so I decided to go for at least a couple of weeks. The Lodin Family were also working at WMPS. That's where I met Sonny Lodin (Sonny James). One of the things I remember during my short stay there was a bass player, John Gollihar, who came from the Knoxville Mid-Day Merry Go Round. John was so smitten with Sonny's sister that he would get weak in the knees when he saw her. I laughed to Sonny about it. He said, "That's nothing new. Every guy that comes along falls in love with her."

Almost as soon as I got to Memphis, Noel Boggs, my steel-playing friend from Bob Wills's band, called me from California and told me they were cutting records day and night to get ahead of the projected union strike on January 1, 1948. He said I could get all the recording work I wanted out there. It sounded good, but I had this old 1941 Packard that I didn't think would make it to California. While I was thinking this over, Joe Allison, a D.J. at WDIA in Memphis, called and said, "How'd you like to work for Tex Ritter?" I asked, "For how long?" He told me it would just be for a few months. Joe was going with Tex on tour, along with Paul Buskirk and Spud Goodall. Now, Spud was a great guitar player but Paul Buskirk was one hellacious musician. He loved the tenor banjo but he was better known as a mandolin and fiddle player. His speed and technique were amazing. He showed me tunings where I could play some real wild stuff.

I left WMPS to go on tour with Tex Ritter. One night, Tex and the band pulled up to a theater in Greensboro, North Carolina. We were riding in Tex's wooden-sided station wagon. We always unloaded the instruments first at the venue, then went on to the hotel and unloaded the luggage. As we drove up to the theater, we noticed it was all boarded up. We drove around to the back and the manager was standing there. He said, "Boys, there'll be no show here tonight." Tex asked him what was wrong. The manager said, "Come on in and I'll show you." The lights were on as we went in. The place was destroyed, seats up by the roots. "What happened?" We all gasped. So he explained it. A magician had been booked with a magic show. This was in the days of segregation and the midnight show had been for the black folks. The manager continued, "This magician had an act where he floated this damn coffin down from the balcony to the stage over the heads of all the folks sitting down there. All went well until that guy sat up in the coffin. When he did, the whole audience vacated the theater, leaving all their possessions behind. It was a mob scene." The manager was right. Our show was canceled that night.

At the theater owner's home in Red Bay, Alabama, 1947.
Back row: Joe Allison, Don Davis, Paul Buskirk, Spud Goodall.
Front row: Dickey Walden, Guynes Walden, and Tex Ritter.

Tex worked with a "high school horse" on stage. Tex had done all his tricks with him—"yes, no" and "howdy" on this particular show. The trainer led the horse back behind the curtain. On the wall back there, between the curtains and the wall, there was this big fire hose with a big valve on it. As the trainer led the horse back there, the horse's butt hit that valve and broke it off. The pressure took over and it straightened out those curtains, washed down the amplifiers and everything on stage before they could get it cut off. It certainly washed all us performers off stage.

We were on tour with Tex playing "Kemp Time," on the Kemp Circuit. T. D. Kemp had a string of theaters. Sometimes these places had nice dressing rooms and sometimes we dressed in a coal bin. We were playing this theater somewhere in the Carolinas and this record executive showed up from Capitol Records, Tex's label. He was a little, short, fat guy named Spence Packley. We arrived at the theater and, as was the custom, started to unload the instruments. We opened the door to the theater and it was pitch black in there. So, ole Spence says, "Boys, I'll go find the lights." This was one of the nicer, bigger theaters on the Kemp Circuit. Spence went in and after a few minutes we heard the darndest crash you ever heard. That poor, short guy had walked off stage and fell in the orchestra pit. We could tell because we heard all those music stands crashing around. We finally found a light and turned it on and Spence came crawling up over the stage. He looked like a coyote that had been in an explosion.

While on tour with Tex, he found out I had this fascination with cowboys from the time I was a kid. I told him I knew everything about cowboys, down to what kind of boots they wore and even what their rings looked like. I had seen all the cowboy movies, paying all of ten cents just to see them. Tex liked this. I told him I was going to California when the tour was over if my '41 Packard would make it. Then Tex said, "Well, you can take my station wagon and use it all you want to."

Tex not only solved my transportation problem, he said that when I got to California, I could stay at his place. I couldn't believe he would have room for me, but he said, "I've got me a travel trailer back there on my lot that's brand new. Bought it to travel in but never used it. Y'all just bunk out there."

When the tour ended, I got ready to leave for California. Spud, who knew his way around Hollywood, decided to go with me. I wanted to take my old Packard to Mobile, but the muffler was broken. I took it to a garage to get it fixed. The mechanic, underneath the car on one of those dollies, rolled his eyes back, looked at me and said, "You one of those musicianeers?" I drawled out a slow "Yeah." Then he said, "My sister married one of those guys. He played clarinet. She finally got tired of him tootin' that thing."

When Spud and I got to California, we found Tex's place. That's where we stayed, 13610 Irwin Avenue, Van Nuys, California, in the San Fernando Valley. Tex's wife was the nicest lady you ever met. Dorothy Faye was so kind to this hillbilly picker. They had a nanny to watch their baby, Tommy, and she used to let me push him around in his buggy. At the time, Dorothy was pregnant with John. (John Ritter became a big Hollywood actor in later years.) You might say I met John Ritter before he was born. Spud never did any work when we got to Hollywood. He just drove me everywhere. I paid him a little and fed him.

I worked sessions day and night in California, just as Noel Boggs had said I would. I don't know how many sessions I did at "scale." We recorded everywhere: in garages, barns, wherever; on wire recorders, acetates, any kind available at the time. I recorded in Buddy Cole's garage. (I remember he brought his baby, Tina, with him, who later grew up and worked on the TV show, "My Three Sons.")

I did a lot of work at Universal Studios. The recording studio was upstairs. I recorded transcriptions there with Ted Lewis. (Remember him? His theme was "Is everybody happy?") He had his entire band with him, but these transcriptions were going to Hawaii, so they needed a Hawaiian guitar. I worked with Ken Curtis, a dude cowboy. He played a while with Spade Cooley and made a couple of B movies. Later he played the role of Festus on "Gunsmoke." I recorded with Foy Willing and the Riders of the Purple Sage. He did a thing where I had to do the sound of a coyote. Foy told me what to do and it seemed to me he knew an awful lot about the steel guitar. Later on, I learned that he really did play steel. So many artists went through those studio doors; I can't remember them all. However, I can't forget that I recorded with Bing Crosby and Dinah Shore. Crosby did "Blue Hawaii."

One day Noel Boggs called and said, "Come up to the studio with me. We need to devise any kind of weird sounds we can come up with. I've got some and I know you fool around with things like that. We are going to record these sounds." We were doing all this for some movie producer. It wound up being the sounds they used in the old black-and-white movie *War Of The Worlds*. That's Boggs and me that you hear making those odd sounds. I never saw the movie, but a lot of people told me about it. That session was the first time I ever saw a real echo chamber. It looked like a grandfather clock on the side of a wall up there. It worked by a great big long spring that went down and they had a unit that put the sound in that spring, then a pick-up at the other end of the spring that caught it. The way they adjusted it to the amount of echo they wanted was by pumping hydraulic fluid into it. When we did all that stuff and they played it back to us, it didn't sound like anything we put down because those engineers had run it through that echo chamber.

Boggs also let me go to a session with him that he was recording on for Jo Stafford, also one with Red Ingle and The Natural Seven. On Ingle's session he recorded the hit "Timtayshun," a take-off on "Temptation." It was a thrill to be there.

From left: Spud Goodale, Paul Buskirk, Tex Ritter, Don Davis.

Recording became so routine, day after day, night after night, I didn't think about it, but when they put me in the studios with cowboys like Gene Autry or Tex Ritter, well, I was so busy staring at them it was hard to remember that I was there to play. These guys were my heroes. Somehow, I was able to come down to earth and do my job. Tex made it possible for me to meet them all, even the actors who didn't sing, like Lash LaRue and William Boyd (Hopalong Cassidy). He took me to lunch with them, letting them all know they were my heroes. I was only 19 years old and still cowboy-struck.

Well, James Petrillo's American Federation of Musicians went on strike, as promised, on January 1, 1948, and banned all recordings with instrumental accompaniment. On January first, I went to the Rose Bowl game and on January second, I left California.

Chet Decker and Don Davis in Hollywood, California.

Howard White - Nashville Airport '50's Berry Field

Steel player Howard White at Berry Field, the Nashville Airport, 1950s.

Chapter 7

THE BOYS WHO MADE
THE NOISE THAT STARTED IT ALL

The union strike ended within a year, but I had returned to Satsuma. One day I got a call from Hal Smith and he said, "Ernest Tubb wants you to come back to Nashville." For some reason, Ernest was unhappy with his band. Leon and Jimmy Short had left him. He thought that Ray "Kemo" Head did not fit his style. Ernest had trouble keeping people steadily in his employment because of his erratic behavior.

I knew this, but I went back to Nashville to play in Ernest's band, The Texas Troubadours. The other band members were Hal Smith, fiddle; Jack Drake, bass; Bill Drake, rhythm guitar; and Butterball Paige, lead guitar. Soon after I came on board, Bill Drake left and Velma Williams Smith replaced Bill.

Early in 1949, Tubb disbanded altogether. He just "cleaned house," keeping only Butterball Paige as a lead guitarist and using local musicians at his road shows. Oscar Davis, his manager, advised this move. Business wasn't as good as it had been. Oscar told Ernest, "I can get just as much money for you and Butterball alone, just let the rest of the guys go."

We were just given away to a new comer at the Opry, George Morgan. Morgan hired us all. The story was that Ernest had arranged it just to help Morgan and us. (Ernest Tubb has never been credited with helping as many people as he helped.) None of us had any hard feelings. I went from a Troubadour to a Candy Kid in the twinkling of an eye. In addition to playing with George Morgan, Little Jimmy Dickens arrived and asked me to play with him on his Opry spots, and WSM asked me to play with everybody who didn't have bands.

After I had been let go by Ernest, on August 26, 1949, Ernest hired me to do a record session with him at Castle Studios. Paul Cohen, A&R at Decca Records, was the producer. We recorded "White Christmas" and "Blue Christmas." Also on that session were Jack Drake, bass; Zeke Turner, rhythm guitar; Billy Byrd, lead guitar; and Owen Bradley, organ.

In those days we all hung out back-stage at the Opry between shows or went to Mom's, later on Tootsie's. There was a lot of camaraderie among the musicians. Earl Scruggs and I were back-stage friends. We go back a long way. Back in the 1940s Earl had an automobile wreck. He was pretty well banged up and was still recuperating from that when I engaged in some conversation with him at the Opry in the dressing room. Since he didn't feel like going across the alley to Mom's place like the rest of us, he kind of sat in the dressing room all alone. Come to find out, he was a real likeable fellow. We didn't talk about music at all. I was never too much of a fan of the banjo anyway, and he probably was not a fan of the steel guitar. I think he was pretty much used to people bragging about his banjo picking. We talked about other kinds of things. We spent several hours talking about anything but banjos and steel guitars.

Backstage at the Grand Ole Opry where Dizzy Dean sang "Wabash Cannon Ball" on stage.
From left: Hank Garland, Dizzy Dean, Don Davis.

Don Davis and
Thumbs Carlisle.

Along about this time I started doing a lot of recording. Before this, country artists had to go to Chicago or Cincinnati to record, or even New York or Los Angeles. WSM Radio engineers Aaron Shelton, George Reynolds, and Carl Jenkins watched this trend for years. Then, about 1945, they put their heads together and came up with a business plan. They pooled their own money, borrowed $1000 from Third National Bank and formed Castle Recording Company. The name "Castle" derived from WSM's slogan, "Air Castle Of The South."

They began it all at the radio station, first with a belt-driven master cutting lathe that etched a mono track onto an acetate disk. They couldn't find room for it at the station, so they installed the lathe at WSM's old broadcast house on 15th Avenue. The mixed signal, played at the WSM studios, had to travel through phone lines to the transmitter building before being recorded. The engineers had to place a phone call to find out if the "take" was good. They would get on the phone and say, "We're rollin'. Are you rollin' out there?" Then we'd hear, "Yeah, we're rollin'!" Then the light would come on. It was a long, drawn-out procedure, considering that we were recording direct to disc.

The new-born recording studio began with a bang. On December 11, 1946, they recorded Hank Williams for New York's Sterling Records. Then in February 1947, they recorded DeFord Bailey on "Pan American." Again in 1947, they recorded Hank Williams with the songs "I Saw The Light" and "Honky Tonk Blues," both becoming hits.

In January of 1947, Aaron Shelton engineered a session for Francis Craig for Jim Bulleit's Bullet Label. In March, Bullet released "Red Rose" as its A-side single on 78 rpm, but it didn't sell. Cal Young, of WKEU Radio in Griffin, Georgia, happened to turn the record over and played the B-side. That B-side was "Near You." Every D.J. in the country got on the B-side after Young. By August, "Near You" had sold 400,000 records and hit #1 on the Billboard charts.

Up to this time, WSM had allowed Castle to rent one of their studios when the station wasn't using it. Then they discouraged this moonlighting venture. So, Castle, with a Number One Hank Williams hit and a Number One Pop hit by Francis Craig, started looking for a new venue. They finally agreed on a former dining room at the Tulane Hotel on the second floor. The Tulane was at Church and 8th Avenue, down the hill from WSM. They had been looking for space nearby so they could slip over on their lunch hour from WSM for sessions. Half the room was piled with unused furniture that the hotel wouldn't move out, so they built a wall around it and then made the space that was left into a studio, a control room with an eight-foot-long window, and a small room for the lathes. Windows let in the traffic noise, so they closed them in with insulation. They placed a few sound baffles around the room, installed a vocal booth and assembled monitors for studio playbacks. They bought an old grand piano and a Hammond organ from WSM. Then they were ready for recording.

The first session I played on was at the WSM studios, in the summer of 1946, with Minnie Pearl. Chet Atkins was also on that session, along with part of Pee Wee King's band. Red Foley had replaced Roy Acuff on the Prince Albert Show and Pee Wee's band, along with Chet, worked with Foley. Bullet Records, owned by Jim Bulleit, hired Minnie for this session. One of the songs we cut was "I'm A'lookin' for a Fella." Chet and I played twin guitars on that. That was the first time I met Chet. He was just a guitar player then. He wound up with the Carters after that session.

Once a month, I was going up to radio station KWTO in Springfield, Missouri, with George Morgan, doing transcriptions for Robin Hood Flour. KWTO was managed by Si Simon. Robin Hood Flour was being handled by an agency out of Chicago, the Thompson Agency. The Carter Family was working at KWTO and I saw Chet again there working with the Carters.

When Castle Studios opened at the Tulane Hotel, I was recording there from the get-go. I did "Country Boy" with Little Jimmy Dickens. In 1949, I recorded there with Ernest Tubb. Also that year I did two sessions at Castle, produced by Art Satherly for Columbia, with George Morgan. On the second session we recorded "Room Full of Roses." Morgan did it first before the fifteen or so other versions. His record went to Number Four on the charts. We also recorded a song I had written, "Ring On Your Finger."

On November 7, 1949, Art Satherly took us to Hollywood where Morgan recorded a duet with Dinah Shore at Radio Recorders. Also on that session were George Van Eps and Perry Botkin, two great musicians. When we returned to Nashville, we did more sessions at Castle. From 1949 until 1956, I did 15 sessions with Morgan; twelve of them were at Castle with Satherly and the last three were recorded at Bradley's Studio on 16th Avenue South, produced by Don Law—all of them on Columbia Records.

I recorded "The Only Boy I Ever Loved" with Carolina Cotton, and "Frosty the Snowman" with the Foley Sisters. I was at a Sunday afternoon concert at Centennial Park on a show when the Foley Sisters performed. Pat Boone was also on the show. Pat and Shirley Foley met there and soon after became an item. I also recorded with Red Sovine for MGM. The song was "I've Got a Lifetime to Regret."

"Sugar Foot Rag" was born at Castle Studios. Paul Cohen called me for a session. He was recording a guy he ran up on, named Eddie Crosby, who sang like Ernest Tubb. Hank Garland was living at Mom Upchurch's at the time and I asked him to go along with me to the session. Hank, who became one of our guitar greats, could also imitate Floyd Tillman. He could sound just like him. When I found out that Crosby didn't have but two songs, I got an idea. Two tunes only made half a session. You always get four songs on a session. Back then, I did a lot of what we called "split sessions," two songs with one artist and two songs with another. I probably got these sessions a lot because I didn't sound the same on everything. They didn't want the same sound on one artist as they had on the other. Somehow, I knew that Cohen was crazy about Floyd Tillman. I told him, "Paul, we need another artist to fill out the session and Hank Garland sounds exactly like Floyd Tillman." Paul said, "He does? Let me hear him." I figured this was Hank's chance. Paul liked him so much, he put him right on the session. Hank sang a song in the Tillman style, "Some Other World." I had been hearing him play "Sugar Foot Rag." He played it all the time, at Mom's, everywhere, so I had him do "Sugar Foot Rag" for the other side. It was released on Decca. From that time on, Hank was "Sugarfoot" Garland. (The Country Music Hall of Fame now has one of those first records in their archives. I don't know what happened to Crosby.)

Hank "Sugarfoot" Garland was a great musician. Living in Nashville, naturally he worked in country music, but also he became well respected among jazz musicians. He was just great. We were both wild about jazz, jamming together every chance we got, playing the wildest chords we could come up with. Naturally, we had our jazz idols, and every chance we got, if some of the greats were playing in Nashville,

Sugarfoot and I were there. After the show we would go backstage to the dressing room. I don't know how, but the guys there had heard of us. We jammed backstage with some of Nat King Cole's musicians and again with some of Lionel Hampton's band. Cole knew his music; he had mastered the keyboard completely, devising a style of his own. Hampton was a remarkably talented musician, playing vibraphone, drums, and piano with a high-powered style of jazz. We were fascinated in the midst of all this real talent.

Somehow, I got invited to play in Memphis with a group of jazz musicians that was playing a benefit at the Memphis Open Air Theater for victims of sickle-cell anemia. This was not an organized band, just a group of jazz musicians that got together for a cause that mattered to them. Slam Stewart, a great jazz bass player who played with a bow, and Oscar Moore, jazz guitarist, were among my heroes of the jazz world playing that night. I was almost a joke to them, I suppose. I was jamming along with them and at one point Oscar commented, "That white boy done laid down a flatted fifth on that Hawaiian guitar." I had really played an augmented eleventh, which sounded like a flatted fifth, but I didn't let on, after he paid me such a high compliment. I just grinned and agreed, "Yeah, man!"

Just being with these greats of jazz fascinated me. I soon learned their backstage recreation was smoking a "joint;" it was part of their culture. They called it a "stick of tea." Their method of rolling that "stick of tea" was unique. They would tear off a piece of a brown paper bag and roll it. Then when they had smoked it down to a nub, calling it a "roach," they took a small match box and fixed it so it would hold that "roach." They called it "putting a crutch on the roach." "Hey, man, put a crutch on that roach," they'd say. They were never shy around me. We were all musicians together. In our world it doesn't matter about color or whether you're rich or poor. We are just musicians, all of us making very little money for doing the work we love. I felt honored they thought I was good enough to jam with them.

Once I recorded with Onie Wheeler for some little label out of Detroit. Onie played harmonica with Roy Acuff, but he was the singer on this recording. The Detroit record man was in the control room at Castle and I saw him lean over to say something to the engineer. Lo and behold, I saw a shoulder holster with a damn hog leg sticking down in it. "Damn gangster from Detroit!" I thought. I guessed that he might own the label. I didn't really care. "Just show me the money," I thought.

I recorded with Hank Williams for MGM at Castle on March 1st and 2nd, 1949, at 11:00 P.M. to 2:00 A.M. One of the songs we recorded was "My Son Called Another Man Daddy." The child in the song was illegitimate, but after we cut it and Fred Rose reviewed it, he decided it needed to be rewritten. Singing about illegitimate children in those days was taboo. Hank and Fred did a re-write. Our cut was unissued. It was not re-recorded and released until 1950. I guess the original is "in the can" some place, if it hasn't been destroyed. We also recorded "Honky Tonk Blues," "Mind Your Own Business," and "You're Gonna Change" on that session.

There have been rumors that Fred Rose wrote many of Hank Williams's songs. Well, I knew then it wasn't true and I learned later just why it wasn't true. When Hank came in to record, his songs were written in a little Blue Horse Notebook. Fred would come out of the control room and look at them. He could hardly see and he would turn that notebook up sideways and say, "That's a good gag." He called a song a "gag." Once in a while he would change a word, saying, "You ought to change this." I know that Hank relied a lot on Fred Rose's opinions and sometimes got help polishing up his songs. I knew that happened then, but later when I got into the publishing business, I found out it was standard practice to help a writer make a song better. That, to me, takes away the myth that Fred Rose wrote Hank Williams' songs. Also, anyone who knew Hank knew he was clever enough to write his own songs. We knew he scribbled down his lyrics just about everywhere he was, especially on those long trips between show dates. Hank wrote a guide for songwriters, published by Harpeth Publishing Co. of Nashville, in which he said, "Carry a small notebook at all times for jotting down chance remarks that might be woven into a theme for a song." Rose was once quoted as saying, "Don't get the idea that I made Hank or wrote his songs for him. He made himself, don't forget that."

A D.J. in Alexander, Alabama, Bob McKinnon, maintains he was an eyewitness when Hank wrote "Kaw-liga." Hank was staying at Lake Martin, an area also known as Kowaliga. Hank said the place was steeped in Indian lore and he felt there was a song in it. Then Bob saw Hank pull out a pad of paper and pencil down the song in fifteen or twenty minutes.

It seemed that I was working with everybody, and when I worked with some of them in the studio during the week, they'd ask me to go on the road with them on the weekends. Well, I figured, they were giving me work in the studios, it was only fair I got out with them on the weekends.

I had just worked my first session with Little Jimmy Dickens and he asked me to play a date with him at a park that weekend. He was traveling in a Buick and he took his wife, Connie, along. Now, I'd never met Connie before. We're riding in that Buick and she looked over at me and said, "My uterus itches." I was so shocked, I didn't know what to say. I looked at Jimmy and his expression never changed. Finally I said, "Jimmy has something you could scratch it with." He's still driving along, not saying a word. Apparently she talked like that all the time. He didn't seem to think a word about it, but it threw me. She was a whing-dinger!

Leon Payne was famous because of his recording of "I Love You Because" when he traveled to Nashville for an appearance on the Grand Ole Opry network show, "The Prince Albert Show." While in Nashville, he recorded his third Capitol session at Castle Studios on Sunday, May 14, 1950, the night after his Opry appearance. He recorded the ballads, "You've Still Got a Place in my Heart," "I Couldn't Do a Thing without You," "If I Could Live My Life Over," and "My Daddy." I played steel guitar on that session along with Dale Potter on fiddle, Zeb Turner on lead guitar, Jack Shook on rhythm guitar, and Ernie Newton on bass. D. Kilpatrick, new at Nashville's Capitol Records, produced the session. Later, liner notes on a Leon Payne re-issue on CD said, "'If I Could Live My Life Over' elicited nice subtle work from Payne and from under-appreciated steel man Davis." Kilpatrick remembers that I was laughing and cutting up on the session, and he told me, "Oh, now let's cut the chatter and get to cutting a record."

Eventually, the big boys came to town: RCA, Columbia, Decca, and Capitol. When RCA first came to Nashville, they had to bring portable equipment because of their union contract. They could not use local personnel or equipment. They used a couple of facilities, all of them bad, before they moved to a studio at 1525 McGavock Street, owned by the Methodist Church—The Methodist Television Radio And Film Commission (TRAFCO) building. (Because none of the makeshift studios had great sound, Chet Atkins opined, "It wouldn't make any difference where we recorded, it was all bad.)

I recorded one session with Porter Wagoner at TRAFCO that was produced by Chet Atkins. After Porter's session, an artist from Atlanta and his band were scheduled for the next session. I was packed up to go when they came to me and asked me to play on their session. They had Pete Drake with them, but Chet refused to let him play. I don't know why Chet did this. Maybe because Pete was then new to him or maybe he wasn't yet a member of the union, but I agreed to play the session. I played Pete's Fender steel guitar. However, I didn't use his foot pedal. When I saw it, I realized it was made from a barn door hinge. That was the first time I met Pete Drake, who went on to become a famous session player, working on many sessions with stars like George Jones and Tammy Wynette.

Eventually RCA built their own studio on Music Row, for several reasons: 1) the engineers had a problem at TRAFCO with bass notes bouncing all over the room, and 2) the Methodists were unhappy because, one morning, after a session, they found an empty whiskey bottle in the waste basket.

RCA and the Bradley Studio, later becoming Columbia, may have been the first state-of-the-art studios, but none of my generation will ever forget Castle. Nobody realizes how many sessions were done at that old studio, all in one room with a control room at one end. I worked there on three or four sessions a day. Once, I cut "Goodnight Irene" four different times in one week; one was for Joe Allison at Capitol. I never told one group what the other one had cut; it was not a good political move to make. Besides, back then, everybody covered each other's songs. There were no albums, only singles. I cut with all the producers: Paul Cohen, Don Law, Steve Sholes, Art Satherly, Chet Atkins, D. Kilpatrick, and some I can't remember. At one point, I was doing so many session, I had a cot put in the studio to get a few winks of sleep.

There was a team of us that did most of the recordings then: me, Dale Potter, Jack Shook, Owen Bradley, Farris Coursey, and Zeb Turner. Also recording there were Harold Bradley, Hank Garland, Billy Robinson, and Ernie Newton. I'm glad nobody came up with the "A Team" idea back then, because I wouldn't want my other musician friends to think they were second-rate just because I was lucky enough to do a lot of sessions. A lot of them were better musicians than I was. (I have heard some of my friends who are on the present-day "A Team" express that same sentiment to me.)

Recording was fun back then. We all played together in the same room. You didn't make mistakes. You weren't allowed mistakes when you were cutting those discs. We didn't have tape yet. Everything was cut on discs, and if a mistake was made they had to scrap the disc and start all over again. Nobody wanted to be responsible for using that time. After all, we needed to get four songs in three hours no matter who the artist was. There was no over-dubbing. The word had not been coined yet.

On August 2, 1955, WSM sent out a memo saying that "all moonlighting businesses would have to be terminated." There were a lot of side businesses going on, from booking to publishing. Some of WSM's staff quit in order to continue their new options. This ended Castle Recording Studios, too, but Reynolds, Shelton, and Jenkins were ready to quit their recording business anyway. George Reynolds had become Vice President and Technical Director of WSM, Inc., Carl Jenkins was studio supervisor of WSM Radio, and Aaron Shelton had become chief engineer of WSM TV. The Tulane Hotel had informed them that the hotel was slated for demolition under the new urban development plan, so they decided to stay with WSM.

As the years passed, so many sessions were done that now they all run together like a blur. There was an album I did with J. D. Sumner and the Stamps. I did an instrumental with Grady Martin, one of the finest guitar players in Nashville. We wrote a song on the session and called it "Slip In, Slide Out." He played the melody on guitar and then told me what he wanted to follow on the steel. (Sometimes, maybe, things are best forgotten.) Owen Bradley produced Slim Whitman and I remember we recorded the song "Rose Marie." A violinist from the Nashville Symphony and I played a duet on that one.

One night on the road with George Morgan, we turned on the radio to Nelson King on WCKY. He played a record and I piped up with, "I sure wish that steel player had tuned up." Then Floyd Robinson said, "Don, that's you playing the steel." I didn't usually criticize other steel players and that's one time I wished I had kept my mouth shut. I suppose when I cut that session, I had done one too many sessions that day. It happens to us all.

Every so often people have asked me what I think about country music today. They started asking me this years ago and it goes on and on. I have an answer for them. The boys and girls that make the noise now are loud and raunchy. They take music and they mix-match it and do all kinds of weird things with it. My thoughts are, "It's selling records." I watch them on TV and they've gotten famous. I say, "Go get it, go get it, more power to you, you're doing a great job." My opinion is that they've taken what we used to do to the next level. If I happen to be someplace and come upon these new artists, I'd like to meet them and shake and howdy with them. Good luck, boys and girls!

Chapter 8

ON THE ROAD WITH MORGAN

Traveling on the road, or even in town, with George Morgan was always, shall I say, interesting. Nobody enjoyed playing practical jokes better than he did, unless it was me. The two of us together were dangerous. Naturally, we always picked on the most gullible of the guys.

We all had nicknames. Morgan was "Whitey," because he was so fair-skinned. Buddy Killen was called "Granny," guess why! Floyd Robinson was "Mousie," because he had a high, squeaky voice. Ken Marvin (real name Lloyd George) we called "Loosh," because he drank so much. Don Slayman had been dubbed "Suds" by an earlier band, because he loved beer. (If he was buying, he drank Falstaff.) George called me "Punk."

Because Suds was a small, nervous, timid individual, he was the butt of a lot of our jokes. Any loud noise scared him. In those days, tires were impossible to get. As usual, we were traveling on "may-pop" tires. Suds was driving, but scared to death one of those tires would suddenly blow out. I was in the back seat. I had this paper bag and I blew it up and popped it. In that closed up car, it sounded like a cannon going off. Suds naturally thought a tire had blown. He steered that car all over the road. He finally got it stopped. When he found out it was only a paper bag, Suds cussed me out with words I didn't know he even knew.

Suds was so little that Goldie Hill gave him a pair of her boots and he wore them forever on stage. One night, Dale Potter and I went into the dressing room and got Hawkshaw Hawkins's boots and hat. Hawkshaw was as tall as any basketball player in the NBA. We put those long tall boots and the great big hat on Suds. The boots went up to his hips and the hat came down to his shoulders. We marched him out on stage while the show was going on. The audience cracked up. They thought it was part of a comedy act. We almost got in trouble for that.

Suds was such an easy victim that Morgan and I decided to really "get" him. Morgan and I roomed together, so we concocted this elaborate plan. For days, I would take Suds aside and tell him that Morgan was in bad shape, very depressed. I told him I was worried. I didn't know what Morgan would do. The band, of course, was let in on what was going on and it added to Suds's worries about Morgan. Then one night, according to plan, Morgan laid down in the bathtub, nude, and I poured Mercurochrome all over his face and throat. Then I put a straight razor in his hand. I called Suds in his room and told him to get over to our room quick, Morgan had done something terrible. The band was all hiding, waiting for the fun to begin. Suds came over on a run and I took him into the bathroom. Suds went in, took one look at Morgan and thought immediately that Morgan had committed suicide. He stood there with tears in his eyes and all he said was, "Whitey, Whitey, you poor son of a bitch." Then Morgan stood up and he and I doubled over with laughter. Suds called us both s.o.b.s then. (This is the true story of the incident. Others have told it with all kinds of variations, such as catsup instead of Mercurochrome, but I was the co-instigator. This is the only version that is the truth and nothing but the truth. Bless little Suds, he is no longer with us.)

There's a story that's been circulating for years about Buddy Killen. He even put his version in his book. I've heard most of the versions, and as any story that's been told over and over, it has become fictionalized. So, I want to set the record straight, since it was mine and Morgan's idea to string Buddy along. At the time I was into drag racing. My good friend, Otis Deck, a drag racer, was my hero. He told me you could actually outrun a car from a dead stand still for just a few feet. No matter how fast a car took off, for just a minute, you could outrun it. A carload of us were riding along to a date, and I got to telling them what Otis had told me. George called my hand on it, so I got out of the car. They counted to three. From a dead stand still, I showed them I could run away from the car for a short distance. Of course, it wasn't but a short minute before Morgan's Cadillac ran off and left me. Then everybody got out and tried to show how fast they could run. Buddy took his turn last. He lived up to his "Granny" nickname. He waited and plotted. He always worried about everything, so naturally we were out to "get" him. We all started putting him on, telling him that he was running faster than he actually was. We told him he was running 25 miles per hour. "Heck," he said, "I can run faster than that." We started placing bets, passing money back and forth. We finally told him he was running 35 miles per hour, before he finally caught on. That's the real story. Honest!

Sometimes things didn't go too well, even for Morgan. Once we were doing a fair date. Everybody was programmed and some guy was supposed to dive out of a tower into a wash tub just before the time Morgan was due to begin his show. Well, the timing was off and we started our show first. We played the introduction and Morgan came out on stage; at the same time this guy climbed up on his tower ready to make his dive. Morgan didn't know this and he started singing and the audience got up and left to see the diver. They looked like cattle heading down the aisle. George looked puzzled. He still didn't know about the man on the tower. Morgan was singing his ass off and everybody was leaving. Loosh said, "You're getting rid of a few of them aren't you Hoss!" George looked so pitiful, but, naturally, we all laughed at his anguish.

When Floyd "Mousie" Robinson and I both worked for Morgan, we both had Oldsmobiles. Somehow, I found out that the key to my car fit his car. On Saturday night, Floyd would park his car in the Opry parking lot and go on into the Opry. I'd go out, take my key and move his car to the other side of the parking lot. When he was done with the show, he'd go out to his car and it wouldn't be there where he had parked it. Of course he would find it, but it like to have run him crazy. I did this to him for about a month.

We were traveling in two cars out in Salina, Kansas, in January, when we ran into a blizzard and got stuck in all that snow. Morgan, Suds, and I were together. Killen, Loosh, and Groucho (Randy Hughes) were in another car. Our car was stuck beside some railroad tracks. We thought maybe a train would come along and rescue us, but no such luck. We had no food, or, as Suds said, "Nothin' t'eat." Finally, after we ran out of gas and were freezing to death, we spotted an old train station off in the distance. We decided to make a run for it or die in the car. I insisted on taking my triple-neck steel with us. We started out, the blizzard still raging in white-out conditions. Suds was hanging on to my belt and in the struggle, I threw that steel guitar out into a snow drift. We finally made it to the station. Morgan was so exhausted he just fell onto the floor. There was an old pot belly stove in there with a fire burning in it. An old man, sitting there, spit tobacco into the flame, looked at Morgan and said, "Is it cold out there, Sonny?"

Lonzo and Oscar were on that tour and the blizzard got them stuck between a bakery truck and a beer truck. They survived by eating cake and drinking beer. (Some people have all the luck!)

After rescuing my guitar, Morgan, Suds and I got to a hotel when the blizzard stopped. Killen, Loosh, and Groucho, in the other car, got in a few days later. "Where've y'all been, good buddies?," we asked. Groucho became unglued. He just freaked out. We let them think we had been there all the time, waiting for them.

Randy Hughes (Morgan called him "Groucho" because his nose looked like Groucho Marx's nose) traveled with us a lot, playing guitar. He was much more than just a guitar player in our business. He managed Patsy Cline and Ferlin Husky. He was married to Cathy Copas, daughter of Cowboy Copas, and he was a friend to all of us. He was also the biggest chance-taker I ever rode with. He was a racing fanatic, and when he was behind the wheel you could count on some exciting moments. I used to travel with Randy quite a bit and occasionally an accordion player, Eggie McEwen, would go along. Eggie and I would sit in the back while Randy sped along at 90 miles an hour, then suddenly pass a car right in front of an on-coming car. I'd think, "Whew-w-w, we made it this time!" And Eggie would say, "Place your bets, boys!" Icy roads didn't make any difference to Randy. He sped along like it was dry asphalt. Randy, bless his heart, always gambled with destiny.

Every time I traveled with Buddy Killen, I nearly froze to death. Once, on a boat, we got caught in the ice in the Straits of Mackinaw and got frozen in. We liked to have frozen to death. They had to send out an ice cutter boat to free us. Another time Killen and I went on a train to New York. We were traveling through a snow storm when the heat quit on the train. Again, we almost froze. I swore off going anywhere with Killen in the wintertime. Morgan thought this was funny.

We used to work up at Bean Blossom, Bill Monroe's park. On this particular show, Hal Smith and Velma Smith were working with us. At the time. Little Jimmy Dickens had a hit called "Bessie the Heifer, Queen of All the Cows." It just so happened that Bill Monroe was there to see the show with his girlfriend, Bessie, who also played bass and sang in Bill's band. Velma was scheduled to sing Dicken's hit, "Bessie the Heifer." She looked out in the audience and there was Bill and Bessie sitting there. Bessie, known as the Carolina Songbird, was on the heavy side. So Velma thought quick and sang, "BOSSIE, the heifer, queen of all the cows."

We were doing a show in St. Augustine, Florida, when we were off for the afternoon and decided to go to a wax museum. Somehow, Morgan got there first, went under the ropes, and when we got there he was standing between the figures of Abraham Lincoln and Ponce de Leon. Morgan, so light-skinned anyway, in that dim light looked like he was one of them. For that performance, we were ushered out.

When we were off the road, we were left to our own devices. Morgan and I were the first to "discover" the Bar-B-Que Chicken Shack on Ewing Drive. It was in a predominately black neighborhood and the hot chicken they served became quite popular; they drew a lot of the white population as well as black, just to eat that chicken.

George Morgan with the lads and a lassie play on accompaniment as he sings and strums as only George can sing!

From the left: Don Davis, George Morgan, Hal Smith, Velma Smith.

Cast of Martha White's Grand Ole Opry show, "'Goodness Gracious,'—It's Good!" 1952. Don Davis is on stage playing the steel guitar.

Front row: Ray Edenton, Don Davis with a National steel guitar, Don "Suds" Slayman.
Back row: Gene Autry, George Morgan, Annie Lou Dill, Danny Dill, Joyce Moore, Bobbie Jo (Allie Oop), Duke of Paducah. *Photo courtesy of the Billy Robinson collection.*

The Bar-B-Que Chicken Shack was owned by a family named Prince. One of the key people in the Prince family was nicknamed "Bo." He served us a lot and we became friends. We found out the reason they called him "Bo" was in reference to the "Bo Dollar." They told us that black people were superstitious of what they called the "Bo Dollar," which is what they called the silver dollar. Silver dollars were circulated a lot in those days, and Bo wouldn't have anything to do with that dollar. He wouldn't take one and he'd leave the room if one was brought in. (Wayne Grove, a coin expert in Nashville, told me that black people still to this day will come in his shop with seventy or eighty silver dollars and ask, "Do y'all take 'Bo Dollars'?")

After learning how Bo felt about silver dollars, we decided he might be superstitious about other things, too. So, we decided to pull a gag on him. We had heard that black people also did not want pig's feet or chicken feet around them. I remembered a gag that Ferlin Husky had pulled and I thought it might make a good gag in this case. So, George and I stopped at a Kroger store and bought a pig's foot at the meat counter. I stuck it up in the sleeve of my coat, holding on to it with my hand and leaving the hoof sticking out. Then George and I went to the Chicken Shack and ordered some chicken to-go from Bo. They got the chicken ready and we started to pay Bo. I had a folded twenty dollar bill stuck in the hoof. I stuck that hoof out to pay him and Bo left—he just disappeared into the kitchen. When he felt more or less safe, he stuck his head out around the door and said, "Y'all can pay me some other time. I'm tied up here, working in the kitchen."

We kept watching how they cooked that chicken in their great big black skillets. We wanted to make it ourselves. I managed to get a sample of that powder they patted on the chicken that made it so hot and delicious. I kind of analyzed that powder and figured out the ingredients. I took my version over to Anna Morgan, George's wife. She had learned how to fry chicken about as well as the Prince family did. A lot of times I'd go over to George and Anna's house and we'd all enjoy that good hot chicken a-la-Morgan. It saved us from having to go down to the Bar-B-Que Chicken Shack. That's how George and Anna got the recipe and how, in later years, Lorrie Morgan, George's daughter, was able to make that good hot chicken at her restaurant called Hot Chicken.com.

I liked to go to a place at 5th and Jefferson called Good Jelly Jones' Good Time House and Showroom. There were a lot of clubs in those days on Jefferson: Dr. Brown's Dinner Club, the Del Morocco, the Club Steal Away, Price's, and the Club Peacock. Jefferson was the Bourbon Street of Nashville. At any time you could find big acts performing, like Little Richard, Jimi Hendrix, Ted Jarrett, or Christine Kittrell. Good Jelly's was my favorite place. It had music, dancing girls, bootleg whiskey, and gambling. It was pretty well known that in Ward One in North Nashville, Mayor Ben West's political allies were led by Henry "Good Jelly" Jones. I talked to Jesse McAdoo and James "Shortdog" Martin recently who remembered Jefferson Street, as it used to be. Well, we laughed and talked about the show girls, or the "hoochie koochie" dancers as they called them.

Off the road and left to my own devices, Good Jelly's was a fun place to hang out. I always sat at the same table on the left in the back of the room where Jesse sat. When I came in, I bought all my associates there at that table a quart of beer. They all knew me and I knew them. One night, after a few beers and watching the dancing girls perform, I got to thinking about a banjo-playing doctor friend I knew. He had a friend who owned an old lion. It had no teeth, couldn't see or hear and had arthritis, but it was tame and wouldn't hurt a flea.

Aha! Inspiration! I wondered what would happen if I took that lion into Good Jelly's and turned it loose. So I called the good doctor, who loved musicians and liked to participate in our fun. We made arrangements to pick up the lion. I put the lion in the front seat beside me. It was fun watching people's expressions as I rode through town. It was after midnight when I got back to Good Jelly's. I parked and let the lion out. We ambled to the door and I opened it. The lion strolled in. Then the folks spotted it. You've never seen people move so fast in your life. People gave way like the parting of the Red Sea. They turned over the beer on the tables in their haste to get away from that vicious beast. Chairs went everywhere. I never saw so many people vacate so fast. The poor old lion was bewildered. I put him back in the car and took him home. A few nights later, when I returned, all my buddies had figured out it was me pulling their leg. I bought them all a round of beer and I became the legend of Good Jelly Jones' Good Time House and Showroom.

I didn't know Hank Williams real well, other than recording with him, but I do remember that once, while I was working with Morgan, we did a show in West Virginia and Hank and Hawkshaw Hawkins were on that same show. Hawk had not come to Nashville yet, he was still working out of Wheeling. He did a whip act where he cut a cigarette or a newspaper out of a person's mouth while it was held with the teeth. He could really do it. Hank Williams was standing in the wings beside me and we were waiting to see the whip act, Hawk's finale. Hawk called a volunteer out of the audience and he discovered too late that the guy was inebriated. He wanted to get rid of him, he didn't want any trouble. But the guy insisted he wanted that paper and cigarette cut out of his mouth. The guy ended up standing there with that spot light shining on him. "Gomer" (Henry Cannon named Hank "Gomer") and I stood there waiting to see what would happen. The guy stood there, in the spot light, weaving back and forth, with that cigarette in his mouth. Hawk cracked his whip and the guy weaved at just the wrong time. The whip hit him right in the middle of his head. Hair flew everywhere, falling like snowflakes there on the stage in the glare of the spot light. The poor guy turned toward Hawk. Hawk's back was turned toward us and Gomer and I had a clear look at the clean spot right across the top of his head. I remember that Gomer had on an orange cowboy suit and he laughed so hard he went right down to the floor. Theater floors are always dirty and he really messed up that orange cowboy suit.

Once, I took George and Papa Jiggs, my stepfather, hunting to Sterling Holt's place. Holt had it stocked with all kinds of birds. I remember very well that we went by Stringbean's house, off Dickerson Road, and borrowed a shotgun from String for George to use. That was the last time I saw Stringbean. He and his wife, Estelle, were killed shortly after that at their own home as they returned home from the Opry. It was a robbery, but the killers never found all of Stringbean's money. It was found years later, in shreds, where String had hidden it, in his chimney. Stringbean did not trust banks.

To be honest, George Morgan and I together were a dangerous commodity. Together we could think up more practical jokes than anybody else. However, I have to give him full credit for thinking up the "Ugly List." He made a list of all the ugliest hillbillies at the Opry. Everybody knew about it. We called it "Morgan's Ugly List." I won't name the ones honored on that list, but all us hillbillies knew who the honored ones were. Those on that list were happy to be so honored.

Bay City, Michigan, 1956. **Standing:** Johnny Tona, Jean Stewart, Joyce Moore, Bobbie Joe (Ally Oop), George Morgan, Annie Lou Dill, Don Davis. **Kneeling:** Danny Dill, Lew Childres, Duke of Paducah, Tyanne Dill.

Recording at the WSM studios.
From left: George Morgan, Hal Smith, Velma Williams Smith, Dale Potter, Curt Gibson, Don Davis.

"Good Jelly" Jones, 1962, who owned Good Jelly Jones' Good Time House & Showroom in Nashville. Jones was Mayor Ben West's Democrat political ally in Nashville. He joined the anti-Metro campaign by carrying carloads of voters to the polls in the charter election of 1962. *Photo courtesy of the Tennessean library*.

Don "Suds" Slayman, fiddler with George Morgan and the butt of so many of our jokes.

Don's steel guitar is a Bigsby, no frets and eight strings on each neck.
The Candy Kids from left: Zeb Turner, Don Davis, George Morgan,
Bob Ross, Joel Price.

WLAC TV POLIO FUND concert. ***From left:*** Dale Potter, Ray Edenton, George Morgan, Don Davis, Floyd Robinson.

Grady Martin's house band at the Ozark Jubilee, 1957. ***Back row from left:*** Frank Horner, Charlie Haden, unknown. ***Front row:*** Grady Martin, Johnny Strawn, unknown, Don Davis playing a Deland steel guitar.

Chapter 9
LUCKY 13

The U. S. Army pointed a finger at me and said, "Uncle Sam wants YOU!" So, on the 13th of October 1950, I answered the call. I did basic training with the 13th Infantry for 13 weeks at Ft. Jackson, South Carolina. If the number 13 seems prophetic, let's say it never brought me any bad luck. I went to school at Fort Gordon and I had just finished that training when the Army opened up an office called the Athletic and Recreation Section (A&R). They kept me there and gave us a building and put in some recreational equipment: pool tables, ping-pong tables, and the like. They labeled me the NCO (non-commissioned officer) in charge of A&R. I had a commissioned officer over me who was never there. Every day I sat around, unless I had to go places and do things that were part of my training. I was given a diploma from the school they sent me to and was called a Message Center Clerk. I had to have a headquarters, so it was at A&R. Then I was sent to school to become a Military Observer and had to go places in order to pass my tests. For instance, I was sent to Smyrna Air Force Base outside of Nashville. I went in there and came out with an aircraft carburetor. I got a diploma there, too. Next, I got a diploma from the Adjutant General School in Indianapolis, Special Services. I did go out of the country one time to South America to do some "looking around."

I figured since the section I was in was called Athletic AND Recreation, it was my job to help the Recreation part. The Army had done their part to comply with the Athletic part, giving us all those table games. So, if I spotted a musician coming through in basic training, I went up to the EPS, talked to Colonel Dubois, and had him pull out the musician and put him in our section, so he wouldn't have to go overseas. We needed them in "Recreation." We got Billy Bowman, Buster Puffinbarger (with Sunshine Sue in Virginia), and Frank Horner, a piano player, and others. One I failed on was Walter Haynes, a Nashville steel player. They wanted him for something else and there was nothing I could do.

All the guys asked me what they were supposed to do and I told them, "Do a show, play some music. That's what this place is all about. Recreation!" So that's what we did. We put on shows for the boys. We had a great band, so we got it all together.

One day, when we were rehearsing, this little Filipino, a supply sergeant named Legeski, came to me and said, "Cpl. Davis, I'd like to be in your show." I asked him, "Okay, what do you do? Do you sing?"

"No. "

"Do you play an instrument?"

"No. "

"Can you dance?"

"No. "

"Well, we'll put you in anyway. This ain't no organized thing."

"What can I learn to do?"

I told him to go downtown to the music store and buy a ukulele. I said it would have a book in it to show you how to play and it will have some songs in it. So he went down and brought back a Martin ukulele. That thing probably cost a couple or three hundred bucks, in the days when you could buy one for $12.95. But it had a book in it and the song "Near You" was in the book.

Don Davis in the U. S. Army, 1951.

The night arrived for our show and we held it right there in the Rec Hall with the pool tables, etc. We all played the show and then I said, "Now here's Sgt. Legeski who's going to sing for you." He came out with that ukulele.

> *Plunk-ah-lunk-ah-plunk-ah-lunk-ah*
> *"Dere's jus' on' place for me Near you..."*
> *"It lak 'eaven to be Near You..."*
> *Plunk-ah-lunk-ah-plunk-ah-lunk-ah*

At Camp Gordon, *From left:* Don Davis, Frank Horner, Billy Bowman.

He got through singing that song and he tore the place up. Those s.o.b.s went crazy in there. I'd never seen anything like it before. I mean, the band had already been in there playing up and down the necks of our guitars, getting down on our knees, trying hard to please the guys and they just half-heartedly went *clap-clap-clap*. But when he got through singing "Near You," they went crazy. That's show biz! You never know! He encored and I brought him back. He said, "But I don't know another song." I said, "I don't care. Sing it again." So he did.

> *"Dere's jus' on' place for me Near You..."*
> *Plunk-ah-lunk-ah-plunk-ah-lunk-ah*

They wouldn't let him off. It was like Lefty Frizzell at the Opry. Here we had the finest bunch of musicians and that little Filipino put us all in the shade. He played a lot of shows after that and he never did learn another song. He got standing ovations every time.

The last man I pulled to A&R was Billy Robinson, a steel player from the Opry. This was just before I was discharged from the service on the 13th of October, 1952. (There's that number 13 again!) The guys never understood why I was gone a lot. They didn't know that the Army was educating me; I was in school, training. The diplomas I got from all those schools have been put to good use; they are hanging on my wall for decoration.

Don Davis and Billy Robinson, U.S. Army, 1953.
Photo courtesy of the Billy Robinson collection.

Chapter 10

THE WILD CHILD

Anita Carter was the daughter of Maybelle Carter. Maybelle was one of the Carter Family who did their original recordings for RCA Victor in Bristol, Tennessee. The Carter style was responsible for the birth of country music as we know it, and it was Maybelle's guitar that defined the sound. After the trio of Maybelle, Sarah, and A. P. Carter split up, Maybelle was joined by her daughters: Anita, Helen, and June. Anita was the first daughter to join the group, then Helen and June followed. So the Carter trio was the same, only better. They were able to reach out to a wider audience without compromising their traditional country sound.

The first time I met Anita Carter was in Atlanta, Georgia, in 1945. I was touring with Pee Wee King then, playing the Atlanta State Fair. I didn't pay any attention to her; she was only twelve and I was sixteen. Instead, my attention was drawn to June Carter, who was closer to my age. I invited June to go on this monstrous roller coaster there at the Fair Midway. I had just gotten off the stage and still had on my cowboy attire, with a Western tie. We took our place on the roller coaster and made it to the first drop. When that thing dropped, June screamed, grabbed my tie and hung on for dear life. She was still screaming and hanging on to that sucker, while my tongue was hanging out, when we came to a stop.

Don Davis and Anita Carter Davis holding the record of "Blue Doll," which Anita performed on Dick Clark's American Bandstand television program.

It was 1949 before I saw Anita again, after the Carters moved to Springfield, Missouri. I was making monthly trips with George Morgan, doing a series of transcriptions for Robin Hood Flour at Springfield. By then Anita was 16 and singing with the Carters. Her voice knocked me out. She was right pretty too, I noticed.

I was a wild child then. I fell in and out of love every three days. I didn't want to settle down to any one female. I had me quite a group of them, the proverbial "girl in every port," or in my case, "a girl everywhere we played."

In June 1950, I was living at Mom Upchurch's boarding house when the Carters came to Nashville—all of them, Mama Maybelle, "Pop," June, Helen, and Anita. When George Morgan and I used to go to Missouri, the Carter family was real nice to us. I wanted to be as kind to them as they had been to us, so I talked all the boys at Mom's into doubling up to make room for all the Carters. I slept on the couch in the living room.

Gene Tierney and Thelma Ritter at the Alabama Jubilee promoting their movie *The Mating Season*, 1951.

Chet Atkins, who had been working with the Carters in Springfield, came to Nashville with them and asked me to find him, Leona, and his daughter an apartment. I found them an upstairs apartment on Granada Avenue in East Nashville. Chet could only afford $50 a week. Chet said, "It was ideal, if we had wanted to live in a sauna. It was in the attic of a little house, with no insulation. The only ventilation came from an exhaust fan used to cool the whole house. And it was June in Nashville!" The only way Chet and his family survived that summer was to spend their days in Shelby Park. By the fall, the Atkins stepped up to a one-bedroom house on Caldwell Avenue, right under the WSM TV tower under construction. In those days, in order to join the Nashville Musicians' Union, someone had to vouch for you. You had to belong to the union to play on WSM and to record, so I vouched for Chet and he became a member of Local 257.

The Alabama Jubilee Band, Mobile, Alabama. *From left:* Don Davis, Doc Gordon, Ben Ford, Roddy Bristol, Jimmy Townsend, and Curly Ganus.

I went into service in October 1950, thus leaving my couch at Mom's and letting her put her livingroom in order. Dale Potter, a brilliant musician, was living there then. Potter was handsome and kind; he could play any kind of music on that fiddle. His talent so impressed Anita that she quickly developed a crush on him. She was only 19 and mistakenly thought she was in love. If she had known Potter very well, she would have shied away from him; Potter was a drinker. Anita realized it too late and the marriage was over quickly.

In 1952, when I got out of the service, I moved back to Mom's. I met up with Anita again and she was so pretty. We started ogling each other and Anita and I married on her birthday, March 31, 1953. That year, I bought a house at 1003 Dew Street in East Nashville, paying $6900 for it. I was able to buy it on the G. I. Bill with a four-percent loan. Payments were $48 a month. That began a regular little clan of musicians in the neighborhood: Walter Haynes, Buddy Emmons, Dale Potter, and Don Slayman.

I played steel guitar on quite a few of Anita's sessions, beginning in 1950, before I left for the service. In August 1950, Steve Sholes produced two sides on Anita at Brown's Radio Productions. We did "Somebody's Crying" and "Johnnie's Got A Sweetheart." I recorded with her again at RCA, on April 19, 1955, and on November 29, 1955. It was on the November session that I met Floyd Cramer for the first time. He was the great piano player who had the hit "Last Date." In 1956, I recorded with Anita again on June 25, March 4, and October 26. In 1957 Anita recorded "Blue Doll" on the Cadence label, but it stirred up only mild interest. The next year, Jim Reeves recorded a male version of "Blue Boy," which climbed into the Country Top Ten.

This brought a renewed interest in Anita's original recording, surprisingly, in the pop field. Archie Bleyer, head of Cadence, called Anita and asked her to appear on Dick Clark's American Bandstand. She agreed and Cadence set it up. After she did the show, I went with her to the office to settle up with Clark's people. Payment for the show was $65. They handed her the check, but they required her to endorse it and give it back to them. I was there with Anita. I swear it happened!

I went with Hank Snow and Anita to have publicity pictures made after they had recorded an album together. They were sitting on a rail fence. Felton Jarvis, A&R at RCA, was there and said, "Hank, move over to the right a little bit." Hank, with never a pause, shot back, "You take the pictures, I'll do the posing."

I tried to stay out of Anita's career, truly believing a husband only interfered. I knew too many husbands who got in the way and the artists died on the vine. Once, I did make a suggestion for a little chord change on her recording of "You Weren't Ashamed To Kiss Me Last Night." They made the change. Felton Jarvis produced it for RCA.

Anita's beauty and talent were unequaled. It makes one wonder just why she never had that big hit, even with so many great producers. There were Steve Sholes, Don Law, Chet Atkins, Wesley Rose, Frank Jones, Jerry Kennedy, Shelby Singleton, Felton Jarvis, Bob Montgomery, George Richey, Don Tweedy, and even Pete Drake. If it weren't the producer, could it have been the fault of promotion? It probably had a lot to do with a bad match between the artist and the song material.

Some think Anita was too tied into her family. She really wasn't free. Word on Music Row was that if you got one Carter, you got them all. There is no doubt that the Carters were a tight-knit family. Anita was also the kind of person who was content to have a seat on the back side of the stage.

I was doing a lot of recording with a lot of people, so when Johnny Bond and Tex Ritter started Vidor Productions, they thought I might be able to pitch some songs for them. They gave me three songs; one was "The Pace That Kills." It was written by Harlan Howard. Kitty Wells cut it and it became Harlan's first commercial release. Another was "Pass Around The Bottle (And We'll All Have A Snort)," also by Harlan. I thought it might be a good Grandpa Jones song, but evidently he didn't think so; he passed on it. The other song was a train song that I thought might be good for Johnny Cash, but he didn't record it.

In 1957 and 1958, when things got lean, I worked some with the Whitey Ford, Duke of Paducah. These were fair dates and a lot of "Boiler Room" shows. Boiler rooms were telephone rooms at a theater that had been previously booked where they sold ads for the program and tickets to merchants before the show. The merchants gave the tickets away to customers. When the ads and tickets pre-sold the show, the show was paid for and everybody was happy. We carried Annie Lou and Danny Dill with us sometimes, or Kitty and Smiley Wilson with Little Rita Faye. Ken "Loosh" Marvin was along, singing "almost" Rock 'N Roll, and Johnny Tona, a fiddle player and pool shark. Characters all! Loosh would stand in front of a mirror and look at himself and tell me, "I look just like Richard Widmark." (A real misnomer!) He also commented, "Johnny Tona has a stance like Rubinoff and he sounds like Harkreader" (an old-time fiddler). A lot of times very few people showed up at these shows. No one cared, as the show was pre-sold. One of these times, Robert Lunn, another Opry jokester and famous for his "Talking Blues," showed up for the show. I looked out front and a man was sitting on the front row reading a newspaper. I thought he looked familiar and when he lowered his newspaper, I saw it was Robert Lunn wearing Loosh's toupee.

Anita and I worked a lot, doing whatever we could to earn money, but by the late 1950s things were changing in Nashville. Sun Records, in Memphis, headed by Sam Phillips, was revolutionizing the music business. A newcomer named Elvis Presley was shaking his way into America's thinking. Phillips was also making stars of Jerry Lee Lewis and Carl Perkins, as well as Johnny Cash. In 1955 the Carters joined a package tour starring Hank Snow, the Louvin Brothers, and comic Whitey Ford. Also booked was Elvis Presley.

The show had been booked by the promoter, Col. Tom Parker—yes, the same Tom Parker who bought me a $27.50 suit when I was with Pee Wee King. Howard White played steel with Hank Snow on that show and he will always remember how Presley's gyrating, on-stage acrobatics had the young girls squealing out front. We had never seen anything like this in a country show. Ira Louvin even went to Elvis and rebuked him for singing such "trash." On this tour, Elvis became smitten with Anita. He followed her around, making a play for her. She told me all about it, not letting me forget it, emphasizing how much Elvis wanted her. I don't know if she was trying to make me jealous or what, but I finally got tired of hearing about it. I told her, "Hey, tell Elvis to come talk to me. We'll work things out." She never mentioned it and we didn't speak of Elvis again.

One day, Col. Tom Parker called and asked me to go out to his place in Madison. He wouldn't tell me what he wanted. So, I drove out on Gallatin Road to see the Colonel. I knew that Elvis was staying out at June Carter's and I wondered if he might be at the Colonel's, too. When I got there, the Colonel told me he was putting a show together and he wanted me to form a band. It was a tempting offer, but I turned him down. It was a short and sweet meeting. As I was leaving, I stopped the car at the gate, waiting for the traffic to clear. I was waiting there when Elvis, on Carl Smith's motorcycle, turned off Gallatin Road and into the gates. He paused for a moment. He nodded. I nodded. He went on in and I went my way. That was my one and only time to meet up with Elvis Presley, the King of Rock 'n Roll.

Chet Atkins, Little Anita Carter, Don Davis.

If that bus could talk! Part of the Alabama Jubilee Band, from Mobile.
From the left: David Boone, Don Davis, Jimmy Townsend, Doc Gordon, Ben Ford.

But it was a sign of things to come. Business was bad in the world of country and western music. The audiences were more interested in the Everly Brothers' "Wake Up Little Susie," or any of the other semi-rock 'n rollers than they were in "Wildwood Flower." The Carters were going in separate directions. You could take the entire Grand Ole Opry to a show date and people would stay away in droves. Suddenly we weren't doing any good here. I knew we had to do something to survive.

I talked to my mother in Mobile and found out she was friends with the owners of a TV station in Mobile, Channel 5. She talked to them about me heading up a live show for them. I met them there and we made a deal. Anita and I moved to Mobile and the show, "Alabama Jubilee," was born. First, I had to get a band together. Mobile had some of the finest musicians playing in its clubs. They were really great, but they were all roustabouts. You couldn't depend on them; they wouldn't show up for work. They were out hunting booze or something. When I started to form my band, I went to the clubs and picked out the musicians I liked. (Everybody told me, "You picked out the best players in Mobile.") I got them all together and said, "Here's the deal, boys, I've got a TV Show lined up and we can get dances. I've got this bus. You will be paid X amount of dollars. But I'll tell you what, pills and drinking is okay by me, but I'm not going to have any drunks. I want you to play music and you can't play music if you're drunk. You might think you're sounding good, but you're not."

The Alabama Jubilee Band appearing for Lee Quality Homes on television Channel 5, Mobile.
From the left: Don Davis, D. A. Gordon, Anita Carter, Don Windle, Ben Ford, and Dee Thomley.

We went into rehearsal and sounded good. I bought a bus and had it rebuilt from one end to the other: transmission, bearings, brakes, engine, and refurbished the inside. It became a nice little Flex bus. I put a cooler in and stocked it with ice and beer. (I wouldn't buy their whiskey.) I got a gallon can of beans, cut the top out, poured the beans out, washed the can and strapped it on the wall back by the wash basin. Now, in 1959, you could buy all the "Old Yellows" you wanted at any drug store. I bought a sack full and poured them into that can. I told them I didn't want anybody out there hunting pills. There were plenty there. Help yourself! And there was plenty of beer. I asked, "Does everybody here have a driver's license?" Yeah, they all did. I took them all down to Trailways to a school to learn how to drive the bus right. I made out a roster, rotating who was to drive each night. Rule Number One was that you don't drink when you drive. The pills were there if they wanted them. But you know, it's kinda like those pigs; stack their food up and they don't want near as much. Same thing with those damn pills. They knew they were there if they wanted them, so they didn't want them near as much.

I had one helluva band. We began playing dances. I had learned a lot while with Pee Wee King and from Hank Thompson. He said, "Hey, don't let 'em come alone to you saying 'he said' or 'he did.' Have a meeting once a week and make them complain in front of everybody." I did just that. I made it Rule Number Two, no drunks on the band stand. They did fine, except once. The bass player wasn't hooking it, so at our meeting I asked him, "What the hell do you want to do that for? You know you're not supposed to play drunk!" He answered with a classic line. "Don, I'm sorry but I'd rather be drunk than president, but I won't do it no more." I had that band for five years and he never broke that promise.

Rule Number Three was always to be on time. If we were leaving on the bus and you didn't get there on time, the bus would leave. You had to get to the date the best way you could. That worked fine until one day I didn't get there and the bus left without me. Well, I had made the rule. They went on to Destin, Florida, and I drove my own car down there. Rules are rules, and I was only two minutes late.

The TV show was from 7:00 to 8:00 A.M. I had enough sense to know people didn't want to watch the same thing every day, five days a week. We covered everything. I'd have guests on the show; we didn't audition anybody. I'd put anybody on and they could do anything they wanted to do. If I didn't have a guest, when a commercial came on, I'd go out the delivery door where people were passing back and forth. I'd stop any old boy and tell him to come over and talk to me. I'd ask him, "Do you sing?" And he'd shuffle his feet and say, "Naw, I don't sing." Then I'd say, "Bet you sing in the shower, don't you." He'd answer, "Yeah, a little bit and around the house some." Right quick I would ask, "What's your favorite song that Hank Williams sings?" "I like that 'Cheatin' Heart' a little bit," he'd say. Then I'd take him into the studio and tell the band, "Hey, he's still got his lunchbox in his hand, but he's gonna sing ''Your Cheatin' Heart'" The red light would come on and the boy would start singing, "Your cheatin' heart will tell on you," and my band would pick up on his key right away. The band would go "pow - pow - pow" right behind me. That band would start kicking and this guy off the street would start singing.

I had people out there every morning. I took a leaf out of Robert Lunn's book at the Opry. I'd make 'em dance, anything. (Robert Lunn, famous for his "Talking Blues," used to audition people in the alley by telling them to sing while standing on one foot and then telling them to lift both feet.) An old lady came by with a sewing machine one day. I sat her up on a stool, turned that machine on and had her sew for us. People watched that show every morning just to see what we were going to do next. We had 70% of the audience in a three-station market every morning. We were loaded down with talent, people who wanted to get on the show.

In between all the amateurs, we had a heck of a lot of professionals who wanted to be on the show. There were song writers Bill Anderson and Harlan Howard. We even had Alan Shepard, the astronaut, and TV actors, Doug McClure and Hugh O'Brien. Dizzy Dean, a huge Roy Acuff fan, came and sang "Wabash Cannon Ball." He used to plug us on the CBS Network "Baseball Game Of The Week" that he announced with Pee Wee Reese.

The Carters—Mother Maybelle, June, and Anita— were on from time to time, too. Ray Sawyer, who later hit as Dr. Hook, sang for us, as did the Everly Brothers. Lots of actors and actresses would ask to be on in order to promote their movies or TV shows, and musicians wanted to promote their records on our Alabama Jubilee show.

We had future hit artists on, too. One, for instance, was Milton L. Brown, who sang folk songs and was beginning to write songs. He wrote one that I thought was pretty good, "I Won't Cheat Again On You (If You Won't Cheat On Me)." I thought it might be good for Ernest Tubb. Now, I knew that Ernest had his own publishing company and needed songs, since he wasn't writing his own at that time. So, I pitched Milton's song to Ernest and the timing was right. He and Loretta Lynn had a duet session coming up at Bradley's Barn in Mt. Juliet, Tennessee. They cut it and Ernest published it at his Ernest Tubb Music, Inc. That was Milton Brown's first cut. He went on to write great songs. His song "Every Which Way But Loose" became the title song in the Clint Eastwood movie of the same name. Eddie Rabbit had a hit record on that song from the movie.

I paid the band for five years and they made good money. We played dances on the weekends in Biloxi and other places. We'd have people lined up waiting to get in. If the club owner asked us to work until 5:00 A.M. for double time, the band would all agree. When we were done, they wanted to go to New Orleans and get drunk. But, according to Rule Number One, the driver didn't drink.

The officials of Mobile would just die to go with us when we went out of town, they wanted to get out of Mobile and let their hair down. I told the police chief, "Don't let any of my boys get a ticket." "Don't worry," he would respond. We had one hell of a good time.

While all of this was going on, our daughter, Lorrie Frances, was born on the 17th of February, 1959. We named her for Lorrie Collins, of the Collins Kids from Los Angeles. Lorrie and Larry Collins were rock-a-billy juveniles who recorded on Columbia. Lorrie Collins was an adorable brunette and a great singer. (Lorrie Morgan was also named for Lorrie Collins.) The Frances part of our daughter's name was for Lew Childres's widow. Lew was one of the Opry's outstanding personalities, called the "Boy From Alabam." The Childreses befriended us before Lorrie's birth.

Our Lorrie's early life in Mobile with Anita and me was probably far from normal. Life is just different for entertainer's children; I was at my TV show a lot of the time. After Lorrie got older, I'd take her with me sometimes and she got to know a lot of the people on the show. Anita still sang with the Carters, and Lorrie stayed with her "Maw-maw" and "Paw-paw" (grandparents) Beard a lot, who were my family. The band and I worked a lot of honky tonks and bars at night and I didn't want Anita to go to those places. Sadly, in the 1960s, Anita and I were divorced and Anita and Lorrie went back to Nashville, living at Maybelle's house in Madison.

I still saw a lot of Lorrie. When Anita went on the road with the Carters, Lorrie came down to Mobile and stayed with me and my family. She was always escorted back and forth on the train. She was never "just left."

"The best we can do" poster for the Alabama Jubilee
television performances of the Dixie All Stars group.

Anita had to be a good person to put up with me; I was quite rambunctious. I had my own career to think about and I really tried not to interfere in her's. She was out on the road a lot. I wasn't bad about fooling around with women, but I did flirt a lot. I wasn't home much and we were very young. It took a while for this wild child to settle down.

WKRG-TV's Alabama Jubilee "talent" show, a woman with a sewing machine and Don Davis.

Poster for The Duke of Paducah show.

Chapter 11
ANITA AND THE KIDS

June Carter was an instigator. She was a close friend of Jan Howard, Harlan Howard's wife. Jan and June were great buddies. June made up her mind to get Anita and me back together, so she got to scheming. She knew that Harlan was a great songwriter. He was writing for Pamper Music, but Jan told her that Harlan wanted to start his own publishing company. June talked to Harlan, telling him, "If you go down to Mobile, you can get on Don's show. Then we can talk to him about opening a company with you." June knew that to get Anita and me back together, she had to get me back to Nashville. So, Harlan went down and sang on my show and June let me in on the fact that Harlan wanted to start his own publishing company.

Harlan and I got together and discussed his idea, and that's how Wilderness Music was born. I went back to Nashville to accept Harlan's offer, but there was another reason I wanted to go back. I wanted to be near my four-year-old daughter, Lorrie. I had bought Anita a house on Cunniff Parkway, off Dickerson Road. I was in a quandary where my daughter would live when the Carters were out of town. So, accepting Harlan's offer settled the question. She could stay with me.

I rented an apartment in a new duplex on Gallavista Avenue in Madison, off Gallatin Road. It had a new driveway of crushed limestone over that nice, Tennessee mud. One night, I woke up at about 11:00 P.M. to an awful whirring noise of someone stuck in my driveway. Min Snow, Hank Snow's wife, and Maybelle Carter were in a Corvair. I went out, got them going, and asked what they were doing there so late. They stuttered around and were quite embarrassed. Years later, we all laughed about this.

As I was back in Nashville, naturally Anita and I talked and, because of our daughter, saw more of each other. She and I just sized everything up one day and, because we had a four-year-old daughter to raise, we came to the quick decision that it was better for everyone concerned for us to remarry. That's what we did. We lived close to music people again. Patsy Cline and her husband, Charlie Dick, lived just around the corner. It wasn't too long before our daughter, Lorrie, had a baby brother, John Christopher, who we called Jay.

Anita and I knew Jay was different when he wouldn't talk. We spent an awful lot of time with him trying to help him express himself. He would jabber and throw temper tantrums at two or three years old. He wouldn't speak in sentences, but he'd say words. Anita put a blackboard in his room and she worked with him a lot, putting his ABCs on the board and making the A and Ah sounds. He was a wonder. He could read and write at three years old. He could look at the dashboard of a car and come home and draw it by memory.

From left: Ezra "Pop" Carter, Maybelle Carter, Don Davis, Anita Carter Davis, Annabelle Beard, J. C. (Papa Jiggs) Beard.

From the left: George Morgan, Don Davis, Reverend Langston, Ezra "Pop" Carter, Anita Carter (Smith), unknown child.

From left: Annabelle Beard (Don's mother), Don Davis, Anita Carter Davis, at their wedding.

From left: Maybelle Carter, Anita Carter Davis
holding her daughter Lorrie Davis, Don Davis.

He was really into car dashboards when he was a little guy. He also liked TV commercials. He wouldn't listen to TV at all, would put his fingers in his ears, but he absorbed what went on in the commercials and then he'd look the words up in the encyclopedia. We had just bought Lorrie new encyclopedias once, and we let him play with them. He would draw little roads on them and put light poles on the roads. He could read but he wouldn't talk much. He seemed never to sleep. He would get on a rocking horse and rock all night long.

When Jay was three, we took him to the Bill Wilkerson Hearing and Speech Clinic to check his hearing. They sent us to a psychiatrist at Vanderbilt University who diagnosed him as autistic. Then, every Saturday we took him to a psychiatrist and a psychologist. We all would watch him play at what he called "Dr. Kaiser's Playhouse." When we left there, we would all go to Minnie Pearl's Fried Chicken. Jay loved the chicken livers there.

We put Jay into a school for autistic children, called Walden House. It was a great school and we spent a lot of time raising money for Walden House. The non-profit school only received a modest part of their budget from state funds. The school set out to prove it could accommodate 19 resident students and 15 day students. In 1971, Felix Barnes and I, on the Board of Directors at Walden House, slated a fund-raising auction of items donated by stars of the Grand Ole Opry and recording artists. One big old boy attending the auction out-bid everyone else for Dolly Parton's dress.

Anita Carter Davis holding her daughter, Lorrie Davis, and proud grandma, Maybelle Carter.

Sadly, what didn't work out the first time didn't work the second time, and Anita and I divorced again. Lorrie said, "I never heard Mom and Daddy argue, never even heard them raise their voices. Mom laughed at Daddy all the time. I remember when folks in the music business thought they were the best looking couple in Nashville."

After our divorce, Anita married a guitar player for Johnny Cash, Bob Wooten, in 1974. (This marriage ended in divorce in 1980.)

Lorrie didn't like her step-father. When she was 15, she moved in with me. I was single and running everywhere. I told her, "As long as you tell me what you're doing, where you're going, and who you're with, we've got it all together." She always checked in with me and I didn't think she ever lied to me. However, as an adult, she told me she only lied about "getting hit on." I got along great with all her girl friends. They called me "Dondee." I liked to take them places like Woolco; I'd make them laugh by walking down the aisles and pretending to be a monkey. I embarrassed Lorrie to death, but her friends appreciated my act.

By 1976, I was the fund-raising chairman for Walden House. Jay was then 11 years old and had progressed to a regular school in the public school system. The kids at Walden House were Number One in my heart, so I sponsored a "Super Concert" for Walden House at the Opry House. Appearing was Jessi Colter, Waylon Jennings, Johnny Rodriguez, and Ronnie Milsap. Dr. Hook was a special guest and

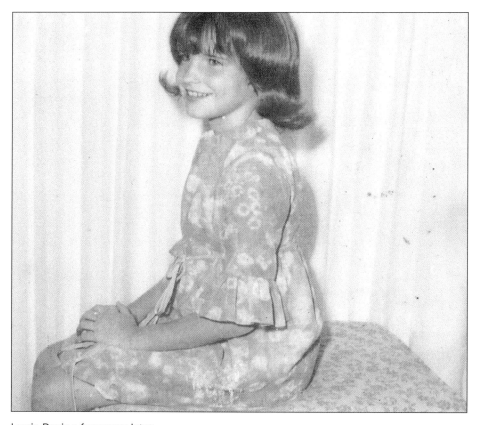

Lorrie Davis a few years later.

Ralph Emery was the host. The artists were not paid for their appearances; all the money raised went to Walden House. Even the stage hands who had known me back in the Opry days showed up without charge—the first time that group of people ever did anything for charity. Maybe they remembered the times I slipped them little airplane bottles (of whiskey) back stage at the Opry. I used to go down to a liquor store on the corner and get miniature bottles of liquor for the stage hands because I felt sorry for them; they didn't get breaks and it was hot backstage.

Jay had special needs, and in cases like these the whole family is involved. Lorrie said her whole life was full of memories of trying to raise Jay, raising money for the school, and taking Jay to doctors. Eventually, Lorrie grew up. She did well in school and the kids didn't realize she was the daughter of a Carter, until her Uncle John, Johnny Cash, had his own TV show and Anita was on the show every week. Lorrie went to the Opry a lot with her mother and sometimes she went to recording sessions with Anita, too.

Lorrie began singing with Maybelle, Anita, Helen, and her cousin David when she was fourteen years old. When she was sixteen, Maybelle got sick and Lorrie didn't work again until she began singing with Anita and Helen. She sang with them until she was twenty-two years old and got married.

In 1990, I married Serilda, a beautiful and kind lady, inside and out. We moved to Gulf Shores, Alabama. Whenever Serilda and I visited Nashville, we always stayed at Anita's house, and Serilda and Anita became very close friends. I'd go to bed at my usual time, but they would stay up until the wee hours of the morning just chatting and having a good time.

Anita developed rheumatoid arthritis, and as she got older there were days when she could not move due to the pain. Her last professional job was for a wealthy man in Atlanta, who requested that she sing at his birthday party. He sent a limousine to Nashville to take her to Atlanta. Her only request was that Serilda go with her, so they made that last date together.

In 1996, Anita made her final recording session with her sister, Helen. This session harked back to their roots in Bristol, Tennessee, as it was recorded near the site of the Carter Family's original recordings and one of the songs recorded Anita wrote while in Bristol, "God Is." Anita's last days were spent in pain. Serilda went to Nashville to be with Anita when she left us to go where "God Is." Lorrie had a line from Anita's song put on her tombstone, "You are safe in the knowledge that you are His child."

After Anita died, I don't think Jay realized that she wasn't just on the road. He refused to go to her funeral. Afterwards, when we took him to her grave, he said, "Mother, I'm so sorry you can't watch Don Johnson anymore." (Don Johnson was TV's Nash Bridges.)

Jay always wanted to please us. He couldn't stand for people to be mad at him. He got frustrated with little things but he wouldn't talk about it. He was living with Lorrie when, one day, after Anita had been gone for two years, he packed his bag and announced he wanted to find his own place. Jay, now 42, has an apartment at Cedarcroft, a home in Lebanon. He loves independent living and is happy, just as Anita wanted him to be.

Anita and I were always best friends; perhaps better friends than we were lovers. Certainly, we loved each other, but as friends our relationship was always strong.

Anita was a wonderful mother to both Lorrie and Jay and gave of herself to them both. She was also a wonderful entertainer and happy with whatever life held for her.

Serilda Davis and Anita Carter at Anita's last public appearance in Atlanta, Georgia. Inscribed, "To my friend Serilda. Didn't we have fun? Hope we can do it again! Anita."

Chapter 12
"Pop" Carter as I Knew Him

The Carter Family, Mother Maybelle, Anita, June, and Helen, were a talented group, but I wish everyone had known the patriarch of the Carters as I knew him. He was a fine guy, a bit rough around the edges, but fun-loving and smart. From the start, we were kindred spirits who got along.

"Pop" Carter (born Ezra, called "Eck" by his family) was A. P. Carter's brother and Mother Maybelle's husband. He and Mother Maybelle were the parents of Anita, June, and Helen. Pop was probably the first to understand how far Mother Maybelle's talent could take them both. He may have been more excited about her music career than she was, particularly after he saw

Maybelle and Sara Carter.

Carter Family records being sold in towns up and down the railroad lines on which he worked as a railway mail clerk. He always seemed to be looking for a way out of Poor Valley, Virginia, where they lived.

I learned that, from the start, he had a gift for invention. He loved everything with a combustion engine: trains, automobiles, or motorcycles. He bought a little house there in Virginia and began making improvements. There was a creek running beside the house and he rigged up a water wheel and ran a generator off it, so that his was the first house in the Valley with electricity. Then he decided he needed a basement to hold a coal furnace, but there was a giant piece of ledge right under the house. He had read about it and figured the fastest, most efficient way to crater-out the basement was with dynamite. Every so often he'd yell, "Everybody out of the house!" Then, "Boom!" You had to move pretty fast. So began his love of dynamite, all because of his need for a basement.

Pop was always fretting over his creek-driven "power plant." Whenever it rained, the dam would go out and the lights would dim. He decided he needed a bigger power plant. He knew a family on a sixty-acre farm on the Holston River about a mile away. He went down there and put a turbine wheel under the river and dammed up the Holston. He got a crew together and they sank twenty-feet-high poles along the entire route back to his house, then strung the electric lines and put in a transformer. After he acquired electricity, the Appalachian Power Company of Bristol bought him out. They paid him exactly what he asked, all the appliances that had been displayed at the Chicago World's Fair. "I don't mean replicas," he said, "I want the actual ones that were there at the Fair." He got them, even the dishwasher. Interestingly, they still didn't have indoor plumbing.

When Anita was born, Pop named her "Ina Anita." The Ina was for an old girlfriend, but Mother Maybelle solved that one problem immediately. She took one look at her baby, called her "Anita," and she was never called anything but Anita.

When I married Anita, Pop Carter and I became great friends. I became pretty well acquainted with him when we lived on Dew Street. He had big ideas and used to come by, quite often, to present me some kind of a big deal he was making on some kind of a machine he was supposedly going to buy. He bought a lot of tools.

He was pretty much of a big spender. He would tell me about some sort of a deal, usually when he had traded-in something. He would present that deal to me using a magic word he always used that was a dead-give-away. "This deal is 'tentative'!" When he used that word, I knew it was a done deal, he'd already bought it. He just wanted my opinion and I'd go along with him. I'd just say, "Yeah, that's the best deal I believe I ever saw. You really socked it to those people on that deal."

Pop Carter told me many stories about his childhood in Poor Valley. Pop (or Eck as he was called) had two brothers, Alvin (A. P.) and Jim. Pop said that in those days, as young boys, they all wore long shirts. That was all they wore, and of course as they were playing and running through the woods those shirts would get up around their waists. Often they would be sent out with a .22 rifle and a cartridge and ordered to bring back something to eat. Folks didn't have much money then, and if they gave you a cartridge, you'd better not waste it; cartridges cost money and were rationed out carefully. One time, the boys had been given their rifle and cartridge and told, "Bring back some meat for supper." They went into the woods way back in the rocky hills and spotted their prey, a squirrel, up in a tree. They shot it, but only wounded it so it fell out of the tree and was scampering down on the ground. It started to run and they chased, planning to club and finish it off. They didn't dare go back to the house without meat. As they ran down the steep hillside, shirts up around their waists, Jim slipped and fell down the hill, landing on sharp rocks. As Pop said, "It tore three cracks in his tail." Jim was pretty well banged up. When they finally secured the squirrel and got back to the house, A. P. decided to medicate Jim. He told him to bend over and hike up his shirt. A. P. anointed the affected area with turpentine. That set Jim off and he started running and howling like a scalded dog. Pop and A. P. ran him down and brought him back, enlisting their Mama for help. She got some cow's cream and smeared it around where the turpentine was to ease the pain. Then, I guess, Mama prepared the squirrel for supper.

Pop told me another story about himself and his brothers. One freezing cold night, they were in their bedroom with a big fire in the fireplace. Of course, there was no indoor plumbing. Jim started having trouble with his stomach and he had a need to visit the outhouse. It was freezing cold and he dreaded going out there. Now, in those days every household owned a lot of crocks. They were used for preserving or pickling or fermenting sauerkraut, and they kept one in their bedrooms in case of emergencies. So, on this cold winter night, not wanting to go outside, Jim played sick. He lay in his bed moaning and groaning. "Oh, Pleasant," (that's what they called A. P.), "Warm up the crock. I'm sick. Can't make it to the outhouse." So A. P. took the crock and stuck the rim of it in the fireplace. He turned it round and round until the rim got red hot. He sat it down by Jim's bed and Jim got out of bed and plopped down on that red-hot crock. He arose immediately, howled, and when they checked him out, he had fried a big ring all around his bottom side. Pop didn't tell me how they "medicated" Jim that time.

Whenever Pop bought a house in the Nashville area, he had a thing about digging up the yard, getting all the rocks out of the yard. He used all kinds of prying tools and dynamite. He had an obsession with rocks that was not dimmed by time or age. It might take him months, but when he got all the rocks out he'd find another place he wanted to live. So, he would buy another house.

He did the spending and Mother Maybelle paid the bills. I was there many times when she was sitting at her dining room table with her check book and all the bills laid out. Pop would run up big bills at Sears. He never bought just one tool, he'd buy several tools of the same kind. He wanted to make sure he had plenty of them. Mother Maybelle would just sit there, writing checks and grumbling. She was a real fine lady, but she would say, "I'm not going to pay this one this time." Pop would tell her he believed in the horn of plenty and I've heard him say many times, "The Lord will provide." It was almost a slogan for him. Mother Maybelle did provide; she paid all the bills that he ran up.

Mother Maybelle and I had a real good relationship. Once, we were in a dressing room and she was tuning her autoharp. I noticed that she was tuning that thing one chord at a time. She'd press down a button for a chord and tune that for a while, press down another button and tune that for a while. I thought this was an awfully complicated way to tune that autoharp, since the thing is simply tuned in chromatics for several octaves. Having the great ear I thought I had, I practically seized it from her and said, "Watch this. I'll just tune this sucker real quick." I thought I could go right down the line and tune it chromatically. I took the thing and started tuning on it and thought I was doing a great job. Then, I found out after messing with it about thirty minutes, the more I messed with and tuned it, the worse it got. Meanwhile, Mother Maybelle was sitting there, quietly snickering at me. I think she had seen that tried before. I learned that I could not tune that autoharp with the great ear I thought I had. Being a steel guitar player, I learned a good lesson from that and I'd like to warn other steel guitar players who think they're great at tuning up steels, with all those pedals and all those different tunings, and have such a great ear. Don't ever take an autoharp away from somebody and try to tune it right quick. I think you'll wind up with egg on your face, like I did.

My association with Pop started off at the Cumberland River before there was an Old Hickory Lake. I had a small, twelve-foot boat, a run-about that Shot Jackson helped me rig up with some controls on it: a steering wheel, a throttle and a gear shift. It was real fast. Pop was real skilled at water skiing. He could do anything on a ski board, moon surf, shoe ski, anything. We used to run up and down on the Cumberland River. We kept on with the water sports after I moved to Mobile Bay, at a cottage, the first place I had down there. My mother was in real estate and sold lots down there. Pop bought a lot just down from mine and built a little shack on it. He spent a lot of time skiing on the Bay. (There weren't any rocks to dynamite out of the sand.) When I'd go down, sometimes he'd run out of money. Mother Maybelle wasn't there to pay his bills, so I helped him out from time to time.

I got to thinking about my association with Pop, watching him blow up things, and I remember that, just before we moved to Mobile, Anita and I had sold the house on Dew Street and moved temporarily out to Pop's house on Tinnon Road. That's where Pop and Mother Maybelle were living then. They had a well and it wasn't supplying enough water, so Pop decided to dynamite that well. He had become a "demolition expert" by then. After all, he had blown up all the yards in the Nashville area. He decided to put dynamite down in the bottom of the well and blow out a bigger cavity down there so he could have a bigger water supply. He drafted me to assist him. The deal was, I would flip the switch in the garage where the detonator was hooked-up. Of course, he got way up on a hill under a tree, where he could signal me. He was way up out of harm's way. When he signaled, I flipped that switch and that dynamite went off and jarred everything around. It put a big crack in the side of his house. Water, rocks, wire and all kinds of stuff flew out of that well about 200 feet in the air. Actually, the project worked out very well. He blew out a big cavity down in the well and he really did have a bigger water supply. The only problem was, the water tasted like dynamite for a long time. The dishes coming out of the dishwasher tasted like dynamite. When they cooked, using water, the food tasted like dynamite.

Of course, there was always a bigger project. Pop had me join in with him on some of his "engineering feats." Once, he bought a place in New Port Richey, Florida. He decided he needed a water supply out there on his boat dock on the river, just off the Gulf of Mexico. The problem was, there was a road between his house and the boat dock. He planned to drive a pipe from the river bank, under the road, and hook it up to the water at the house, so he could have a water supply on the dock where he cleaned his fish. He devised a hydraulic rig where we hooked up water to try and jet that thing under the road. So, I was driving the pipe under the road with a sledge hammer and doing real well, until it got to the middle of the road and it was harder to move the pipe. I kept hitting it harder and harder, just shutting my eyes and bearing down harder. It stopped, but I got it moving again. Then, I ran into a stump or something, down in the ground underneath the road. That pipe curved up and came through the asphalt paving. We had a big water fountain spewing there, so we had to withdraw the pipe.

Dixie Hall told me this story. Before she was married to Tom T. Hall, she was Dixie Deen and she lived with the Carters. Pop Carter persuaded her to go with him on a trip to seek out some public domain songs. This was a big thing that was going on then. People were taking those old songs that were in public domain, recording them, and copyrighting them under their own name. Pop had a little bit of an eye for business, a way to make extra money, so he enlisted Dixie who was at the time a journalist for *Music City News*. He took Dixie along to the Ozark Mountains with the idea of recording some old songs they might be singing up in those hills. They were driving along and spotted an old lady up on a porch, singing with a guitar. They set up a machine and recorded that lady for a long time. Pop got all her songs on tape and had a big smile on his face. He asked her, "By the way, Ma'am, where did you get all those songs? They're mighty fine songs we got on tape here." She grinned and said, "Off a Porter Wagoner album." So much for Pop's adventure into public domain land! (Of course the songs on Porter's album were all copyrighted, but the lady had no idea of the difference between a copyrighted song and a public domain song.)

These were just some of my experiences with Pop. According to the Johnny Cash books I've read, he regarded Pop as a spiritual leader. I respect his opinions, but my ideas of Pop are quite different. Pop went about religion in his own way. He was a reader. He had a collection of books on science, electricity, aviation, and religion. While they still lived in Poor Valley, Mother Maybelle took the girls to Mount Vernon Methodist Church. Pop, being curious, would follow and stand outside under a window and listen to the preaching and singing. Once, he crawled under the church to listen. One Sunday he went in and was baptized. But that didn't mean he ever attended services. Pop and I didn't talk about religion. We spent most of our time on skis, blowing things up, and having a few shots of Jack Daniel's together. I got along fine with him and all the Carters. There never was a finer lady than Mother Maybelle.

Chapter 13
HARLAN

I remember well when, in 1964, Harlan Howard and I started Wilderness Music in an old house in Nashville, at 913 17th Avenue South. We refurbished it on the inside and our plans were that Harlan would write songs while I would record demo sessions and build our catalog. I surely became busy; we would do as many as eighteen songs in one session. We opened Wilderness as a Broadcast Music, Inc. (BMI) company and Harlan was a BMI writer. Most publishers had both a BMI company and an ASCAP company, because BMI writers could not write for an ASCAP company and visa-versa. BMI gave us an advance of $100,000 to start and we never opened an ASCAP company.

Until 1930, song publishing had no presence in Nashville. It was done in New York, Chicago, or Hollywood. The American Society of Composers, Authors and Publishers (ASCAP) was organized by Victor Herbert, but it barred writers who had no formal musical training or a Tin Pan Alley (New York) pedigree. That presented country music publishers with a problem, since ASCAP was the sole conduit through which songwriters received royalties for song performances. Radio stations signed contracts that allowed them to play unlimited ASCAP songs for a blanket annual fee. In turn, ASCAP distributed royalties to its member publishers and writers. Yet, ASCAP would not accept blues, folk, or "hillbilly" songwriters as members, consequently prohibiting those writers from prospering. This promised a bleak future for country music writers. This situation might have continued, but ASCAP sparked a war among radio broadcasters and suddenly radio was cutting into sheet music and record sales. Therefore, ASCAP argued, their writers were entitled to more than they were getting from radio. Their contract with radio was nearing expiration in the late 1930s, and ASCAP proposed a doubling of royalties or no ASCAP music would be played on radio.

This jolted the radio men. They refused to pay and the negotiations got nowhere. When the expiration date, December 31, 1940, came and went, radio could no longer legally play any ASCAP song on the air. This period ushered in songs by writers such as Stephen Foster, who were deceased and whose songs had long been in the public domain (songs whose copyrights had expired). Those songs got their greatest exposure then. "Jeanie With The Light Brown Hair" was played often, in fact it was played so much that a running joke emerged that "Jeanie" would get The Song of the Year Award.

Signs for the Wilderness Music Inc. (Harlan Howard) and Twitty Bird Music Publishing Company (Conway Twitty) being set up together by L. E. White and Don Davis.

The National Association of Broadcasters, with Neville Miller as head and Edwin Craig on the board, created their own performing rights society, Broadcast Music, Inc. (BMI). It was launched in 1940 and they began building their own music catalog. BMI opened its doors to writers without music reading tests and a few unhappy ASCAP writers and publishers. When radio stations pulled ASCAP music off the air, country music skyrocketed. BMI was able to give country music a home and collected millions of dollars in performance fees for the country publishers and writers. By the time the ASCAP ban ended, BMI had amassed 36,000 songs from 52 publishers.

In 1955, Frances Williams (now Preston), a WSM receptionist, was asked to set up and run BMI's southern regional office in Nashville. She worked from her home for three years before opening an office in the L&C Tower in 1958. By 1964, a striking new BMI building was erected at 10 Music Square East.

Debenture certificate for Twitty Burger, Inc., 1970.

Finally, in 1962, ASCAP embraced country music and Nashville, after learning that there was "gold" in the hills there. Juanita Jones ran ASCAP's office during their first Country Music Week in Nashville. They didn't have a country song to give an award to, so Juanita went to the WSM library to hunt for an ASCAP song worthy of an ASCAP Song of the Year Award; but it didn't take ASCAP long to catch up. Now, they have their own building at 2 Music Square West. There's a saying in Music City, that "It all begins with a song," so it is only fitting that both the BMI and ASCAP buildings are the first you see when approaching "Music Row" (originally 16th, 17th, and 18th Avenues South).

When we formed Wilderness Music, our "hillbilly" hearts were still with BMI. We remembered their loyalty to us and were loyal to them. At that time, I knew music but I didn't know anything about "song plugging," that is, pitching songs to artists or producers for recording. I watched Harlan work and learned a lot from him. I went to Burl Ives's room with Harlan and Hank Cochran and watched them work. We didn't have the songs on tape, but just sang them "live" with a guitar. Hank Cochran, from Pamper Music, was a great songwriter and a champion song plugger. He just wouldn't give up. When an artist arrived in town, he'd be the first to move with the artist until session time. I caught on, and watched him and Harlan all I could.

Soon after we opened, Buck Owens blew into town. He and Harlan were old friends and Buck was "hot" at the time. Buck and Harlan took off for Printer's Alley and, while there a'sittin' and a'drinkin,' they got an idea for a song. Harlan came in the next day all excited and said, "Man, Buck and I wrote a hit last night, 'I've Got A Tiger By the Tail.' Buck's gonna record it." "Oh, boy," I said, "I guess we got publishing." "Well," Harlan said very slowly, "I've got to tell you what happened. We flipped a coin and we lost." So Buck's company, Blue Book Music, published it. Well, at least Harlan got royalties for his fifty-percent of the writing, so he didn't lose. He knew he had a tiger by the tail, that was plain to see.

Wilderness became a magnet; people from everywhere came. We'd do a demo session and the next morning, at 8:00 A.M., Billy Sherrill would be sitting in his office at Epic waiting, because I had promised him I would bring the session over and let him pick what he wanted for his artists first—and I would. A&R men often tell their secretaries to tell a song plugger to just leave the tape. I never left a tape with anybody. We didn't sign writers exclusively, we just signed their songs. After all, Harlan Howard was exclusively ours.

Wilderness was the fulfillment of Harlan's dream to own his own publishing company. He already had hit songs that were once just a dream. He grew up in Detroit listening to the Grand Ole Opry.

His favorite singer was Ernest Tubb. Harlan would go around singing Tubb's melodies, and if he couldn't remember the words he'd make up his own. The radio was his teacher. He had a ninth-grade education and then entered the military. When he got out, he worked factory jobs in Detroit and Tucson. In 1955 Harlan was working in a Tucson lumberyard and had saved enough money to buy an old car to take him to Los Angeles where he got a job driving a forklift in a factory. He kept writing songs when he got off work; he often drove his old car down the freeways to publishing companies in Hollywood.

One afternoon, he walked up to some offices and saw two men dressed like cowboys sitting in an office, with their boots up on the desk. They happened to be Tex Ritter and Johnny Bond, who had just started Vidor Publishing. Harlan went in and said, "Got me some songs I've written." Tex said, "Well let's hear 'em." Harlan just had a cheap guitar with him and he played and sang three of his songs. They impressed Tex and Johnny so much that Tex told Harlan to put them down on tape and bring them back to them. So Harlan did. Tex and Johnny believed in Harlan's songs, so they tried every angle to get a cut ("recording" in music business lingo). They even gave me three songs to pitch in Nashville to try to get cut.

According to Joe Johnson, then with JAT Music (Johnson, Autry, and Thompson) in California, one day, Tex Ritter, who was a friend of Gene Autry, came to him and said they had just signed some songs with a new writer, Harlan Howard, and needed to give the writer a $100 advance. Tex said that if Joe would give him the hundred dollars they needed, they would give JAT Music one-half of the publishing. Joe gave them what they wanted and became co-publishing owner of "I Can't Hold a Memory in my Arms." Nothing seemed to be happening for Harlan. Knowing that Joe at JAT had put money up for his song with Tex and Johnny, he went to Joe himself. Joe Johnson said, "I signed 15 songs of Harlan's to JAT Music; one of them was 'Above And Beyond.' I recorded Wynn Stewart on that song in 1958. Wynn had a monster. Then, when Buck Owens got a record contract, he recorded it too. 'Above And Beyond' became a classic." (A later recording was done by Rodney Crowell.)

One night, Harlan was in a club called George's Roundup when he saw a couple fighting. When she left, the man hollered, "Well, pick me up on your way down!" All Harlan needed was an idea and he went home and wrote a song. One day, he called his friend Hank Cochran at Pamper Music. Hank told Harlan to send him a tape and he'd pitch Harlan's songs with his songs. Hank pitched "Pick Me Up On Your Way Down" to Ray Price who knew that Charlie Walker, then a D.J. in Texas, was looking for songs. He played it for Charlie, and Charlie cut it. It became an instant hit. But Harlan wasn't ready yet to quit his day job. As yet, he had received no money.

Finally, one day, he got a check from Pamper for a sizable amount. Three days later, he got another check for even more money. He bought a new Cadillac Coupe de Ville, a fancy new guitar, quit his forklift job and moved to Nashville. He wrote so many hit songs from then on that it's impossible to name them all. Just a few were "Heartaches By The Number" (Ray Price), "I Fall To Pieces" (Patsy Cline) co-written with Hank Cochran, "Life Turned Her That Way" (Mel Tillis), and "The Blizzard" (Jim Reeves). In later years he became known as "the Irving Berlin of Music Row."

Wilderness became like Grand Central Station. I might walk in to see Hank Cochran leaned up against the wall, or Roger Miller cracking jokes, or Willie Nelson strumming his old guitar. Bobby Bare would stop in just to soak-up the atmosphere. Once, Bobby's house caught fire and was badly damaged, so I moved him with his family out to my house. Bobby recorded a song of Harlan's called "The Streets Of Baltimore" and it became a big hit.

All of us looked forward to *Billboard Magazine* each week. We all sat around and waited for it to arrive so we could find out where our songs were on the charts. One week, Bobby was out of town on tour and he called me to see where his song was on the charts. It was somewhere about 16 or 19 and going up, but I told him it went down to 20, with a bullet. There was dead silence on the line for about a minute. Then all Bobby said was, "Shit!" That's all he had to say before I busted out laughing and told him it was moving up to the "Top 10."

Wilderness got going so fast it was scarey. We kept five songs on the charts all the time. When the money started coming in, real money, I said to Harlan, "What are we going to do with all this money? We can't handle it, we need help. I want to keep my mind on music. I'm not about business." Harlan asked me, "What are we going to do?" I said, "Let's sell half this thing to Tree" and he agreed. I knew Buddy Killen and Joyce Bush at Tree very well, so I went around the corner and talked to Joyce. We made the deal right then. They administered all the business and after that all we did was music. Nothing happened in our office but the music.

Fred Carter, Jr., played on our demos a lot and he was a great guitar player. He went along with getting our demos done in a timely manner, instead of getting hung-up on one song. We depended on him. Fred was the man who was instrumental in the album "Bridge Over Troubled Water," that Paul Simon and Art Garfunkel recorded. When they came to Nashville to visit, Fred invited me to his house to join them. I sat down on the floor and enjoyed the evening as Fred played the guitar and Simon and Garfunkel sang their songs.

I got so that when I played a tape for somebody in the office, I could tell by the expression on their face how they felt about the song. In one case, I was playing songs for a know-it-all wise guy, a real intellectual. I wasn't getting any reaction, so I stopped the song right in the middle of the tape and said, "Man, I want to apologize to you for playing that tape. That song would really be a tough song to sing, it has so much range in it. You might have a tough time with it." I began to fast forward to the next song. He stopped me right there and said, "Wait a minute. Run that tape back. Make me a copy of it. I can do that song." He cut it that afternoon at a 2:00 P.M. session. Boy, did I "rope-a-dope" him!

We signed some songs from Lola Jean Dillon, a little girl from Moss, Tennessee, who was only 18 years old. She turned out to be a pretty successful writer for us. Her first successful song was recorded by Dolly Parton on Monument, "I've Lived My Life and I'm Only 18." It did well in the charts. She also wrote "In the Park After Dark" for Norma Jean. The biggest that she wrote was "When the Tingle Becomes a Chill" for Loretta Lynn. It went to Number One.

Lola Jean said that in those days she didn't know anything about the music business. She and her husband, who raised chinchillas, would go by the radio stations and plug her songs. She was a real "country" writer and a singer. She and L. E. White, who wrote for Twitty Bird, wrote and recorded songs together. They had some success with "The Vacation" and "You're the Reason Our Kids Were Ugly." After seven years, she moved on to write for Loretta Lynn's company, Coal Miner's Music. From her Celina, Tennessee, home, Lola Jean said, "I must have written two or three hundred songs."

June Carter hung out a lot at Wilderness with Harlan's wife, Jan. One day, we wrote a song together, "Adios Aloha." We did the demo at Cinderella Studios, owned by Wayne Moss. Joe South played guitar on that demo before he became a hit artist. One of the recordings of that song was by The Canadian Sweethearts, Lucille Starr and Bob Regan. Lucille sang what she remembered to me by phone from Las Vegas.

> That's all I have to say,
> Adios, aloha, 'hasty lumbago'
> And a buenos noches to you...

When the house next door to Wilderness came up for sale, June and I talked it over and decided to buy it for an investment. We made an offer on the property, filled out the contracts and paid out our earnest money. The real estate agent was Little Roy Wiggins, who had been the steel guitar player for Eddy Arnold. A few days later, I asked Roy when we would close the deal. Roy said, "I'll tell you what, some people came along and offered more money and I took their offer." Well, he took their offer after he took our earnest money, so we were thrown out of the deal. Our "investment" fell through.

June and I, always business-minded, concocted a venture for a short while called CARDA Productions (Carter-Davis). The objective was to send out a reel-to-reel tape with news of Nashville on it to the D.J.s. We talked about what was going on in Nashville, who was seeing whom, and who was getting two dollars, that sort of thing. When we sent out the first editions, the radio stations jumped right on it. They really wanted to sign on and buy the deal. About that time, June and Johnny Cash got together and the idea silently slipped away.

From time to time, some of the artists would want to start a publishing company with Wilderness. We couldn't accommodate them all, but we did start one with Conway Twitty, called Twitty Bird Music, (BMI). I first met Conway in early 1965. Harlan asked me if I had a steel guitar around and I told him there was an old one in a closet somewhere. Harlan said, "Well, pack it up. We're going to Muscle Shoals, (Alabama) to Fame Studios and record some Rock 'n Roller who thinks he wants to sing country." So we did. The song the boy cut was "If You Were Mine To Lose," a song he wrote. Guess who that Rock 'n Roller was! Yup, it was Conway Twitty (Harold Jenkins, his real name). Harlan took the session to Owen Bradley at Decca and the rest is history. Rock 'n roll lost a star to country. We had a long association with Conway after that. His Twitty Bird Music was housed upstairs in our building.

We also started a company with Waylon Jennings, in about 1965, that he called Baron Music, (BMI). Waylon had been working in Phoenix and recorded with A&M Records. Sometimes he used the name Waylon Jennings on his recordings and sometimes he used the name Jackson King, which we made fun of. When he first came to Nashville, he was rooming across the alley at Sue Brewer's place (Sue kept boarders). He approached Harlan about getting him on RCA and Harlan got that done. Then, Waylon signed with Lucky Moeller's Talent Agency. He started his own band, so he needed a bus, equipment, band uniforms, etc. I took him to Commerce Union Bank where I had a good friend, Joe Marchetti, a vice president. I showed Waylon's RCA contract and his booking contract to Joe, who loaned him the money so that Waylon could work the road. Then, Waylon gave me a picture of himself and autographed it this way:

> *Don, when I came to Nashville I was penniless but thanks to you, I now owe $100,000. But you're still in there swinging.*

A sure way to get songs recorded is to produce records, so I began producing a few records myself. The first step is to pick the songs for the artist. I was getting ready to produce Lefty Frizzell, and he and I were listening to songs one night. He'd left word with his wife, Alice, to forward any calls he got to the office. The phone rang and it was a call to Lefty from an operator at one of the clubs he was going to work. Lefty and I were having a big time listening to songs and "partaking of the grape"– a little vodka, if I remember right. Lefty took the call from Texas somewhere. The operator told him the boys in the house band had learned all his songs and had all his keys squared away. Lefty had a sidekick named Abe Mulkey who sang tenor with him and went with him on all his dates. The operator asked Lefty if he was bringing anybody with him and Lefty said, "Yeah, I'm bringing Abe Mulkey." The operator said, "A monkey! Lefty, don't you bring no monkey down here amongst all these drunks. They'll go crazy. They'll tear this place up. Don't do that!" Lefty said, "No, no monkey! I said Abe Mulkey!" The operator said, "That's what I thought you said, a monkey!" By that time I had a drink half way down and I got to laughing and almost choked to death, listening to Lefty and that operator talking.

Both Lefty Frizzell and Dallas Frazier were friends who used to hang-out at Wilderness, and they were notorious for getting sick when they got drunk. So, one day I got them in the back seat of a car, took them over the roughest stretch of road I could find and gave them warm beer to drink. Eventually, they started making loud, moaning, crying noises. They hollered, "Pull over, I'm sick." I recorded it all and that cassette tape made the rounds of Music Row for a while.

Connie Cato was one of the artists I produced for Capitol Records. We were doing a song called "Here Comes That Rainy Day Feeling Again." What I wanted was a Sonny James sound on the guitar, so I called Sonny and asked him if he would help us. When I arrived at the studio, Sonny sat waiting for us with his guitar. That single became a hit, and there's no one as generous as Sonny James.

Motown Records called me one day and wanted to know if I could find a black girl who could sing country. I had just the girl for them, Ruby Falls (born Bertha Dorsey). They wanted me to bring her to Los Angeles, so Ruby and I took a plane to meet with them there. We had to change planes in Dallas, and as we got off in Dallas, there stood Janie Frickie and the Gatlin Brothers. They said, "Hey Don!" I said, "Hi guys!" "Where ya goin'," they asked. They eyed Ruby and me with suspicion; Ruby was very pretty. "I'm taking Ruby to L. A. to sign her with Motown," I said. "Sure thing, Don. We know," they answered me. They didn't believe a word I said, I could tell. They thought I was getting out of town with Ruby. No amount of explanation would have made it any better, so I didn't explain further. Motown did sign Ruby and I produced two sides on her, "I've Never Been Kissed There Before" and "Cracker Jack Jewelry."

Harlan used to hang out at Sligo Boat Dock, on Center Hill Lake. This was a gathering place for people in the music business. Usually, you could find Harlan, Mel Tillis, Porter Wagoner, or Curly Putman there, among others, swapping fish stories. They did a lot of "night fishing." They called themselves "Going Fishing Together." There was a zillion miles of shoreline at Center Hill Lake and they all went in separate boats and kept in touch by C.B. radios, like walkie-talkies. Once in a while, they'd stop and visit with each other. There were all kinds of stories about those boys circulating around. They drank a lot of coffee and told all kinds of strange stories about UFO sightings and other strange things. I think they might have used a lot of those "old yellers" up there.

Harlan was back in the office after one of his trips to Sligo, when a package came for him. He opened it and found a case of cans of coffee. There was a note in there from Curly Putman. "Sorry, I bothered you, but here's some coffee to replace the coffee I bummed off of you." Apparently, Curly came by Harlan's boat in the middle of the night and bummed coffee off Harlan. Everyone up there carried a big thermos of coffee in their boats. Harlan made some off-hand remark about it that offended Curly and he took it seriously. Harlan said, "How can I handle this? I didn't mean to offend Curly. I need to send it back." I said, "No, don't send it back. Here's how to handle this. Send back two cans with a note saying, 'Curly, you didn't drink that much coffee. I'm returning two of the cans.'" Harlan did that and everything smoothed over.

One night, Porter Wagoner and Mel Tillis were fishing when one of those rockets the government was experimenting with misfired and exploded in the air over Center Hill Lake. Porter and Mel thought that God had sent a sign that this was the end of the world. Mel said, "P-P-P-Porter, the Lord's c-c-coming! Q-q-quick, throw the pills overboard!" And Porter did! Now that's why I think the old yellers played a big part in their strange sightings out over the lake.

The Sligo Boat Dock is in a cove off Center Hill Lake, about 70 miles from Nashville. In those days, a lot of country music entertainers had what they called "boat houses" tied up there. These were fitted out like little three room cottages, on top of pontoons. You might call them "hillbilly house boats." I had Harlan's permission to use his boat anytime, so one Friday afternoon I decided to spend the weekend at Sligo, doing a little running around and sightseeing.

The Weather Channel had not been invented yet, so I didn't know they had had one hell of a storm there the night before with lots of wind and rain. When I arrived, expecting to find Harlan's and Porter Wagoner's boat houses next to each other at the dock as usual, Porter's boat house had come untied during the storm. Fortunately, the guys at the dock had managed to save Porter's boat house from going down stream by tying it to Harlan's.

It was blocking my entry, so I untied the rope thinking I would retie it in another location. But, despite all my efforts, the rope slipped away from me and I could not retrieve it. That's when I realized Porter was still inside his boat house and, thanks to me, he was unaware that he was now on a ship without a navigator.

When I finally got Harlan's boat house under way, I think I passed Porter adrift on the lake. Later I learned that a friendly fisherman towed Porter back in.

True confession time, Porter! If you're listening, I swear I didn't do it...on purpose! Bon voyage! (Later boat houses were outlawed. The Corps of Engineers, in their infinite wisdom, made the "Center Hill Navy" disband.)

Music publishing companies earn royalties from BMI from radio airplay. I knew that radio stations logged what they played with BMI, and that's how we got our airplay money. After we had a lot of records in radio land, I made a catalog of all our songs, putting down the information for every one and mailing it to the D.J.s with a note, "This is for your convenience when you log for BMI, so you won't have to look up all those records." We also did a mass-mailing to the stations for our records that came out. It's a huge job, stuffing and addressing envelopes to every country D.J. So I went to the Florence Crittendon Home, a place for unwed mothers just around the corner, and arranged with the lady in charge to let me hire some girls to stuff and address the envelopes. We had a list of radio stations from the CMA and we sent records to all those program directors.

A lot of the program directors would call me. They didn't usually respond to publishers, but they remembered me from when I was beating the road as a musician. The D.J.s from little radio stations used to knock on the back stage doors, and I always was nice to them, letting them see the show. Through the years, these little D.J.s had become program directors and they called me to say, "Hey, I remember you and we're going to play your record." That made me feel good. We got a lot of air play money from BMI because we mailed our catalog and made their jobs easier.

The music business is a learning process. One learns by doing what you can't learn in school. Just as I had learned what a good song was and how to pitch songs from Harlan, and how to produce sessions, after I had spent countless hours producing demos, I also learned tricks of the trade from promoters I had worked with.

Chapter 14
JOHNNY CASH

When I first met Johnny Cash, he had not yet become a legend. He had some hits under his belt, but it takes a while to get "legend status." At the time, I was pitching a few songs for Johnny Bond and Tex Ritter's publishing company. One of the songs was a train song. I was working on the Opry at that time and I was married to Anita Carter, June Carter's sister. When I got to the Opry one night, Cash was back stage. I had heard Johnny's song on the radio, "I hear the train a'comin', it's rollin' 'round the bend." I didn't know it was about a prison. I'd only listened to the train part. I went up to Johnny and said, "I've got a train song you ought to hear." He said he would like to hear it and said, "Let's go out to your house after the Opry and listen to it." I thought that was strange. I'd never met the guy, but why not.

We started out Shelby Street to Dew Street where Anita and I lived. Johnny wanted to stop for cigarettes, so I pulled into Troy Lynn's Drug Store on Shelby. I remember the brand he bought, Picayune. When we got to my house, I found out he wasn't interested in my train song, only that I was married to Anita Carter, June's sister. Somehow he knew that I was June's brother-in-law and he was interested in getting close to June. At this time, Johnny and June were both married to other people. I found out later that he had introduced himself to June that night at the Opry by saying, "Hello, I'm Johnny Cash and I'm going to marry you someday." That was the night I met Johnny Cash. He neither heard nor cut my train song, and I've even forgotten the name of it.

Because June Carter was my sister-in-law (my family), I was always trying to help with her personal problems. When she and Carl Smith split, it nearly killed June. Carl became infatuated with singer Goldie Hill. I do understand why Carl took a liking to Goldie. She was a beautiful and personable woman. I worked with Goldie a lot doing Opry spots. Her two brothers, Tommy and Kenny Hill, were really good friends of mine, so we had a good friendship going.

However, the break-up was very hard on June. One day at WSM, on the Noon Time Neighbors show, June fainted and I picked her up, put her in the car and took her to Madison Hospital (then Madison Sanitarium). I carried her upstairs to the emergency room and sat with her for awhile. One Saturday night, after the Opry, she was distraught and the Carters were going on the road. She asked me to take her to her home in Madison. I did and sat by her side all night long, consoling her. Sometime after that, she stayed with me for a couple of days while the Carters were out of town. I comforted her as best I could. One day, she walked out on the front porch and a neighbor, thinking she was Anita, called out, "Hi, Anita." June and Anita did look a lot alike. June and Anita laughed about this for a long time. June was like my sister and I always tried to be kind to her. I'll always be glad we had that closeness.

When June married Edwin "Rip" Nix about 1962, I really liked Rip and he and I became good friends. Then June and Johnny Cash became real friendly. I didn't think June ought to be involved with Johnny while she was still married to Rip, my buddy. Then, of course, June and Rip split. The next time I really got with Cash was when June called and wanted Anita and me to spend some time with them at Don Pierce's farm in Hendersonville, on the Old Hickory Lake. We went out there and, as guys will do, John and I left and went to a black club in Gallatin that he knew about. We didn't stay long, had a couple of beers and went back to Don's.

Well, June Carter Nix and Johnny Cash got married in 1968, in Franklin, Kentucky. That made John and me brothers-in-law. Anita and I wanted to get them something entirely different. There was an old man who had a shop in Bellshire, a suburb of Nashville. He had a huge and ugly chair, all hand-carved, that looked for all the world like a throne. I tried to buy it, but the old man wouldn't sell. I had a collection of old clocks, old mantel clocks like Seth Thomas clocks. I offered to swap the clocks for the chair and he traded, then and there. We gave the chair to John and June, and John kept that chair until he died. Every so often, I would see an album cover or something with John sitting in that ugly chair. That's how Johnny Cash and I became friends.

Cadillac car given to Don Davis by Johnny Cash for producing his hit song, "One Piece At A Time." **Standing:** Don Davis and Stonewall Jackson.

Don Davis driving his Cadillac.

One day, I was driving down 16th Avenue South when I heard a song on the radio that excited me. It was a duet by a song writer I knew, Billy Edd Wheeler, and a girl, Billie Joan Scrivner, called "Jackson." It occurred to me that it would be a great song for June and Johnny.

As usual, I wanted to help June. So June took the idea to Johnny and they began singing it on their shows. One night, Billy Edd was on the same show with Johnny and June in Asheville, North Carolina. They sang "Jackson" and the crowd went wild. When Johnny saw Billy Edd back stage, he told him, "Whenever the show seems to bore the crowd, I call June out and we sing 'Jackson' and they go crazy. One day, we're going to record it." Billy Edd told me that he told Johnny, "That would be great!" But inwardly he was thinking, "If you like it so much, why do you put off recording it." Billy Edd told me he was sitting at a bar on Music Row when Kris Kristofferson came in and sat down beside him. He and Kris had never met before, so Billy Edd introduced himself. Then Kris got all excited, saying, "Billy Edd Wheeler! I was just at Columbia Studios and Johnny Cash and June Carter just recorded a hit song of yours — 'Jackson.'" When the record was released, it became an instant hit. Johnny and June collected a Grammy for the best Country and Western performance by a duo for "Jackson" that year.

I was in my office when Shel Silverstein, from New York, came in to see Harlan and me. He wanted to start a publishing company with us. After talking to him, we decided that Shel was a little too much for us, so we turned him down. Then Shel said, "Hey, let me sing you a song I just wrote." So he did. It was different. The title was "A Boy named Sue." In Chapter One of this book, I tell the story of how I got this song to Johnny Cash and the outcome of his live recording at San Quentin. "A Boy Named Sue" became the best seller of 1969, and I still feel a thrill for my part in getting that song to John.

Once I heard John on Larry King's show on CNN. King asked him, "How did you find "A Boy Named Sue?" John thought a moment, then replied, "Well, some buddies of mine, Kris Kristofferson and Shel Silverstein, were having a 'guitar pulling' and Shel played me this song he had just written. I knew it was a hit when I heard it." Now John knew better than that. He's been quoted in at least six books in which he told the real story. Maybe he thought this was a better story for the Larry King show, or maybe he had put too many logs on the fire, but John knew that I knew. What's more, June also knew the truth.

By 1974, Harlan and I had moved our offices into the Tree International offices. I hadn't been there too long when John called me. He had been having some extremely lean times. "Don," he said, "Can you come up with another hit song?" I guess he thought he'd better call me to find another hit. I got to rambling around up there at Tree and found a Joe Tex song called "Papa's Dream." It knocked me out; I loved it and talked to John. He listened to the song and said, "Hey, I like that, but can we change the name?" I asked him what he wanted to change it to and he said, "Look At Them Beans." Well, I talked to Buddy Killen, as he produced Joe Tex. Buddy said he wouldn't ask Joe to change it. So I called Joe. First, I asked him if it would be all right for us to get a cut on "Papa's Dream." He said, "Yeah, man, it's all right with me." Then I asked him, if Johnny Cash was going to cut it, could we change the name? He said, "All right with me, man!" So I gave John the okay. John called me about a week later from his studio. He said, "Don, we're having trouble with this thing. We can't come up with a thing. Can you come out here?" I told him I would, but I added, "It'll take more than just your band, the Tennessee Three." And John said, "Do whatever you want to do." I hired a band and singers, made music arrangements and went out to the House Of Cash Studios and produced the session on "Look At Them Beans" and a couple of other songs. John liked it and sent me to CBS in New York with the tape. They were happy with the project. When "Beans" started going up the charts, CBS wanted an album, so I gathered up a bunch of songs and we recorded an album.

When "Look At Them Beans" hit, John called me and said we had to decide what to release next. We had recorded a song for the album written by Dave Kirby, "What Have You Got Planned Tonight, Diana." So, the big question was what to release next. I felt we should release the "Diana" song. In other words, pull a switcheroo, something different, a change of pace from "Beans." John said, "I'll think about it." The next thing I knew they had released a song called "Texas Forty-Seven." It went nowhere and John went down again. Then Merle Haggard released "Diana" and guess what, it went to Number One. I had produced a successful album on John and we were proud of it. So John did his usual thing. First, he let the piano player who had been on the "Beans" session produce him. Then he began to let anybody and everybody, whoever, produce him. And again he hit a dry spell. Then John called and said, "Don, do you think you can come up with something else again?" So I went through the songs and found "One Piece at a Time." I asked Buddy Killen what was happening on that song. "Well," Buddy said, "Mercury has signed this boy, Wayne Kemp, a singer/writer, who writes for us. He wants to do that song." I said, "I can probably do it with Cash. You'd make a hell of a lot more money." Buddy told me I'd have to talk to Kemp. I found him at a honky-tonk in Texas. When I explained to him that Cash might want to do his song, Kemp laughed and said, "You know I was told this tale about this plane mechanic who made off with enough material, a little bit at a time, to build a helicopter. I thought it was a funny story, true or not, and wrote 'One Piece at a Time,' substituting the Caddy for the 'copter. Sure, go ahead, give it to Cash."

Front cover for Johnny Cash's album "Look at them beans," produced by Don Davis.

I took John into the studio at House of Cash and recorded "One Piece at a Time." Gene Ferguson, the promoter, happened to be in the studio. After we were done, John went over to the engineer, Charlie Bragg, and told him we need to "pull one out of the can" for release (meaning a song recorded previously and not released). Ferguson blew up. "Have you lost your mind?" John said, "What are you talking about?" My whole world was swimming past my eyes. I had talked Buddy and Wayne out of that song, and now John wanted to put it in the can. Ferguson spoke up again, "John, you just got through cutting a smash!" Gene Ferguson saved the day! They released "One Piece at a Time." He just happened to be there. It became Johnny's best-selling single since "A Boy Named Sue." It stayed on the charts for fifteen weeks and at Number One for two weeks. I was the producer, but every time they release that song they tacked on a co-producer, Charlie Bragg, that engineer who would have passed on the release. However, deep in John's heart, he knew who to thank. He gave me a brand new 1976 Cadillac Brougham and, as he said in *Billboard Magazine*, "to show his appreciation for bringing him his latest hit."

Picture taken in Jamaica with a Polaroid camera.

Now, that is the true story of how "One Piece at a Time" was recorded. In a recent biography about Johnny Cash, an individual was quoted, telling his version of how "One Piece at a Time" was recorded. This person said that Cash left the session after putting down a scratch vocal. After Cash left, the musicians worked out the instrumental track. Then later, Cash came back and, with help from this person, put his voice on the track. Well, that's a complete untruth. I want to counter that by saying I produced that record in its entirety, and as a matter of fact, all the Johnny Cash productions that I produced, and completely directed it. I did all the musical arrangements and told the musicians what and when to play. This session, as all the others, was completed when Johnny Cash was there. At no time did Cash come in and sing later. There never was a time when tracks were laid down and vocals were put on later. They were all done on the spot. I was in complete charge and no other person had anything to do with it or helped in any way.

I do remember some of the musicians and singers I used on Cash's sessions, for instance Joe Allen, bass; Johnny Gimble and Tommy Jackson, fiddles; Jimmy Tittle, trumpet; Earl Ball, piano; Curly Chalker, steel; Hurshel Wiginton and Delores Dinning, vocals. As usual, I always included the Tennessee Three, Marshall Grant, Robert Wootten, and W. S. "Fluke" Holland.

I knew Cash for many years, but our direct contact wasn't frequent; we had a casual relationship. We always got along fine when it came to business, but we didn't socialize that much. Once, I took him with me to Bon Aqua, Tennessee, to Sterling Holt's farm. Holt had several acres up there that he stocked with quail, pheasant, and all kinds of birds. He owned dogs and you could go there, give him fifty bucks, and he would take you on a bird hunt. He liked you to bring two or three more hunters and he would take you on a four-hour trip and you could shoot all the birds you wanted. His dogs would find the birds and flush them out. So, one time I took Cash up there and we had a good bird hunt and a real big time.

When I produced a record for him, we never had problems. Sometimes he called me for my opinion or advice, usually about the music business. He'd need to talk to someone who would give him honest advice. Sometimes, it would be about legal problems, and he might ask me if he should bring up a matter to his lawyer. He did call me when Pop Carter died; he wanted my advice about who should serve as pallbearers and I told him that nephews are always a good idea. He seemed to trust my ideas regarding songs (particularly after "A Boy Named Sue"), but he would go for a long time with just so-so songs before he would call me.

When Cash started House of Cash Publishing, Pop Carter called me and asked if I would get together with Cash and run it for him. I never knew if Pop made the call on his own or if Cash had him call me, but I turned the offer down because I was too deeply involved with Wilderness at that time. Even though Johnny Cash was my brother-in-law, we did not have strong feelings toward each other, one way or the other, and that was probably a good thing. Personal relationships get in the way of a good business fellowship most of the time.

In September of 2003 Johnny Cash, the legend, slipped away from us. June had died barely four months before. Their grave site sits atop a small hill in a cemetery in Hendersonville, not far from their lake-side home. Nearby are Maybelle and Pop Carter. Anita is also there. In my heart they were all legends in their time.

Chapter 15
THE TREE YEARS

We spent ten good years at our offices on 17th Avenue South. One day in 1974, Jack Stapp and Buddy Killen at Tree talked to us about moving our offices up to the Tree building. I thought it would be a good idea. I was starting to do some producing and Tree owned a studio I could use and a vast access to songs. Harlan and I agreed. We learned from our accountant that the IRS had a rule that a songwriter, who owned a certain percentage of the stock in a corporation and his copyrights contributed a certain percentage of the income of the publishing corporation, became a personal holding corporation subject to 90% tax. Harlan approached Stapp and Killen at Tree and said, "Why not give Don a big bonus instead of giving it to the government?" They all agreed and I thanked all concerned.

The Tree name was such a draw in the music business worldwide that all kinds of artists came through those doors, from just about everywhere in the world. It was a great publishing company to be affiliated with. There were many outlets for songs, not just for recordings, but for movies, television, and more. I never knew who might show up in my office.

One day, Buddy Killen brought Paul McCartney and his wife, Linda, into my office. Buddy was hosting the McCartney's visit to Nashville. Lee Eastman, Paul's father-in-law and Buddy's attorney, had asked Buddy to do this as he thought Nashville was an ideal place to inspire Paul to write some new songs for his new band, "Wings." Buddy talked Curly Putman, a Tree songwriter who had written "Green Green Grass Of Home" and other great songs, into loaning the McCartneys his 133-acre farm in Lebanon, for a nominal fee, for their stay here. On this particular day, Buddy introduced Paul and Linda to me, then left to attend to a business crisis. I welcomed them and sat Paul in a chair and Linda at my desk. I told Linda I had a great idea for Paul and myself. "You know," I said, "Paul and I would make a great team, like Dean Martin and Jerry Lewis. Paul sings, he can play the Deano part, and I can do comedy, and play the Lewis part. Paul, with his English accent, and me, with my Southern drawl, would be a natural." Linda obviously didn't know whether to laugh or cry. Paul barely suppressed a laugh. "Don't you think so?" I asked. Naturally I was only kidding, but they didn't know it. Luckily, Buddy showed up and rescued them. They left as I was saying, "Nice to meet y'all."

After Kitty Wells left Decca, I produced a record for her called "Does Anybody Out There Want To Be a Daddy," written by Dave Kirby. We did the session at Woodland Studios and a group of Tree writers was sitting in the studio giving advice. After each take they'd say, "Do it again!" I finally got a take I liked and told the engineer, "It's a wrap." The writers were still saying, "You need another take." Walter Haynes, a producer from Decca who was there, quietly said, "Put it out there. They'll let you know." They were words of wisdom. I've never forgotten Walter saying that. The engineer made me a rough copy and all the writers clamored for a tape copy. I said no, as I never liked to make anyone a rough copy, no matter how much hell they raised. Even if they thought it was a hit, it was not yet a finished product. I didn't want copies out until it was finished.

Along the way I learned that if I do a session and all the musicians start raving over it, I get worried. If they leave the studio looking sad, shaking their heads, I think maybe I've done it. The next day, after all the hurrah, just to be a nice guy, I took my rough copy by Curly Putman's office so Dave Kirby and the others could hear it. Their appraisal was, "You've done it again. It's a hit."

I didn't know then, but there was another Don Davis in record land. He was an African-American producer from Stax Records who produced Johnnie Taylor. I was producing Lawrence Reynolds, who was from Mobile, Alabama, and we had a hit going, "Jesus Was a Soul Man." Reynold's record went into the pop charts, as did Taylor's. My name, as producer, was in the billboard charts at the same time as the other producer Don Davis, who got static from Stax, thinking he was producing for another label. He called me saying, "Hey, you gotta help me, brother." I didn't hear from him again until 1976 when I had the hit on Johnny Cash's "One Piece At A Time." He had a big hit with Taylor, "Disco Lady," on CBS Records. Taylor was from Crawfordsville, Arkansas, and CBS held a big convention in Hollywood at the Century Plaza Hotel at Century City, California, and invited both of us. As I was walking down the hall at the hotel, I met the other Don Davis. Johnnie Taylor was with him and Taylor was really inebriated. Davis said, "Johnnie, I want you to meet Don Davis here." Well, poor old Johnnie just came unglued. He looked at me and then at the other Don Davis, one white, the other black, and he could not believe what he was seeing or hearing. Then he sank right down to the floor, completely done in.

I was the clown at the parties I attended in the business. I became known as the "Chicken Man," because of my "cold call" telephone conversations regarding chickens with the rich and powerful. It wasn't always my fault, but there was always a bunch of wine drinkers egging me on. For instance, one night, we were out at Fred Carter, Jr.'s, Nuggett Studio having an "after session" party. Frances Williams Preston, of BMI; Fred Foster, of Monument Records; Buddy Killen, from Tree, and a whole bunch of people Harlan Howard had rounded up were there. As the evening wore on, we all got silly and Fred said, "Hey, Don, let's call somebody and you do your chicken act." After some discussion, we decided on Percy Cohen, a prominent businessman who owned Cohen Furniture Store. (We knew we had become somebody in this business when we could afford Cohen furniture.) It was late at night and I called him at home and the conversation went like this:

"Sir, this here's William Jackson down at the loading dock of REA Express. We got some over shipments down here and we gotta move this stuff out. We gotta shipment here for you."

Cohen cut me off curtly with, "I accept all my shipments down at the store."

"Sir, I can't keep this stuff down here. We're not allowed to keep poultry and livestock over night."

"What do you mean, poultry and livestock?" He almost screamed.

Don Davis and Connie Cato in the recording studio.

Front and back covers
for Lawrence Reynolds'
album Jesus is a Soul Man,
produced by Don Davis.

Car representing Johnny Cash's hit song, "One Piece
At A Time," produced by Don Davis. **Left to right:**
Charlie Bragg, Johnny Cash (driving), Don Davis, Ron
Bledsoe, and Kirkpatrick, the junkyard owner.

Producers Don Davis and Don Davis in a former
Motown studio in Detroit.

"We jus' can't keep it, sir, we gotta get it outta here tonight."

"Well, what is it?"

"It's chickens, sir!"

"CHICKENS!!!!!!!!! Ah-h-h, no, no, no!"

Cohen then threatened, "You come on my property and you'll be trespassing.
I'll shoot you!" I hung the phone up and we had a big party.

Now, here we are at the studio. They have me in a room rigged up to a mike,
plugged into a speaker, and all the guys and gals are down in the studio listening
and laughing.

The next day, I walked in the office and there was the biggest, ugliest dang rooster
I ever saw in a cage. At one time he had been white, but now he was coated in coal
soot. It didn't have feathers on one side; the other side had lots of feathers. Fred
Foster had sent him to me. After we all had our laughs, I gave him to a guy who
lived behind our office on the alley, in a little shack with a smoke stack on top. The
next day, the old guy said, "I boiled him and ate him all'.'

One night, after Harlan and I and some other writers had spent most of the night listening to songs and had had a few drinks, they begged me, "Come on, Don, do your chicken act for us." We knew that one of the all-night D.J.s had a call-in show for people with problems. So we decided to call him.

I said, "I'm a referee for the Bankruptcy Court."

"Yes, you're on the air." (He was very nice.)

"I've been here many years and I run into people who really do act ugly. I try to deliver stuff from a now-bankrupt company that used to ship to people by rail. We have lots of stuff left over at the loadin' dock at the train station."

The D.J. says, "Uh-huh."

"Some of these bills of ladin' are old. I call 'em up in the phone book and when I call 'em they say we didn't order that there. One lady and man got in a fight over which one ordered 'em. One man even shot at me."

"Shot at you?" The D.J. sounded shocked.

"Yessuh."

"What were you delivering?"

"Five hundred chickens, suh. You see, they used to be baby chicks, but because they have been here so long, they all growed up. We been feedin' and waterin' them for a month or so."

The D.J. laughed. "What are you going to do with five hundred chickens?"

"I just don't know, suh. They said I could have 'em, but unless the peoples signs somethin' to release 'em, they might say I was stealin'."

"That's an incredible story!"

"I appreciate your listenin'. Do you have any advice?"

"Folks, if you see a man delivering chickens, please don't shoot him."

[Note: Many of the people working in the music business caught this act at different times, like Polly Edenton at Decca and Leslie Elliott at Sho-Bud. They will attest that these events happened.]

After those stories, I have to admit that I had inspiration for doing my chicken act from Jolly Joe Nixon. He was a popular D.J. in Los Angeles, originally from Old Hickory, Tennessee. Joe was connected with some Hollywood notables and involved in the music business. Joe came into town with Ann-Margret and Roger Smith, her husband. Joe started all this chicken business and I fell right in with him. When he got to town, we immediately went up to Joe's room and made our usual "chicken calls." Roger Smith was in the room and he urged Joe to tell me what he had done to Lee Hazelwood in California. It was a right interesting story.

It seems that Frank Sinatra presented Lee a new Ferrari because Lee had produced a hit for Nancy Sinatra, "These Boots Are Made For Walking." (Jolly Joe was in cahoots with Lee at the time, into publishing and production.) Joe saw Lee's Ferrari parked in the parking lot and, being the practical joker that he was, devised a plan. He brought a five-gallon can of gas into work with him, and every time Lee parked his Ferrari, he went out and filled the tank back up. After a while, Lee mentioned to Joe, "Hey, man, this Ferrari beats anything I ever saw. It's got a great big 500 hp engine in it and it doesn't burn any gas. I drive it all the way into town from out where I live and it doesn't burn any gas." Finally Joe said, "Let's go down and look at that car. This is unbelievable!"

They went out to the parking lot and Joe said, "Pop the hood and let me see what's going on." Lee popped the hood and Joe reached down under the hood as if he was doing something. Then he said, "There it is!," and slammed the hood back down. After that, Joe quit putting gas in the car. One day Lee came into Joe's office and said, "Hey, man, this Ferrari is drinking gas. It's only getting six or seven miles to the gallon. Go down there and whatever you did to it, undo it. This thing's ruining me."

I learned a lot from Joe. I only saw him baffled once. He had come into town with Ann-Margret and her Hollywood people. We were in his room and Joe was getting a lot of calls. He had put his calls on a speaker phone. One call came from a representative of the Tennessee Walking Horse Association. He wanted to know about the possibility of making a movie about Tennessee Walking Horses. Now, Joe, being a quick thinker, said, "Well, sir, it probably would cost you about twenty-five million dollars just to start making a movie like that. That's an educated guess." There was a pause. Then the guy said, "About twenty-five million?" Joe said, "Yeah!" The guy replied, "Well, that's no problem." Joe didn't know what to say then. He was completely baffled. When he hung up I said, "Well, we can't handle the walking horse people. Let's get back to making chicken calls."

Things were going along great. Life was just fun and games. Then I met a girl who ruined it all—for a few minutes. It all began one night after a Johnny Cash session. All of us regrouped at a wrap-up party at the King of the Road Motor Inn bar. I took a girl with me and Hurshel Wiginton, bass singer on the session, brought a girl with him. I didn't see either girl again, until one day Hurshel's girl showed up at my office. Her name was Eva Charline, but she was called Charley Ann. She was a beautiful girl, shapely, and looked like Suzanne Somers. She worked for Cosmopolitan Spa, but she was a wannabe singer and song writer. That should have sent up a red flag right then, but she was so kind, really nice to me, washed and massaged my face, very attentive.

Then we got married! The day we got married she tried to take control of my mind and soul. I took a break and we went to Gulf Shores for a couple of weeks vacation. She still tried to tell me what I could and couldn't do. One day, I came in and she was starting to cook. She turned around and accused me of sleeping with another woman. She said, "You've slept with every woman in Nashville." I said, "Yeah, but Nashville ain't all that big." That's when she hit me in the head with the skillet she had been holding in her hand. We split soon afterwards. I wrote her a check, kissed her good-bye, and put her on her way. I thanked God and Greyhound she was gone.

The hardest thing I ever had to do was tell Harlan Howard a song he wrote was no good. I was producing a gal from Mobile, Boots Till. Harlan brought me a song, "The Gay Divorcee." Now I was faced with the problem of telling the greatest country writer of all time that this song was not a hit. That is no-man's land. Nobody told Harlan that! I was always the first to hear Harlan's songs and, like any other writer, he wrote some bad ones. Songs were Harlan's babies, you just couldn't say, "That's a bad song."

When Harlan would say, "What do you think, Don?" I had a standard reply for a less-than-good song. "Well, Harlan, that's just not a Harlan Howard song."

Harlan would then say, "You don't think so?" "No, it's just not a Harlan Howard song." He'd say, "Okay," and in the trash it would go. That's how I got by with not accepting a Harlan Howard song.

The day came in 1977 when we decided to sell our business Wilderness to Tree. Harlan and I agreed we had done as much as we could do. Harlan had hit a dry spell; most writers do. He got the feeling that he had written himself out. However, out of this depressing time, he wrote "No Charge," recorded by Melba Montgomery. I had gotten to the unenviable position of becoming Harlan's "personal secretary," handling all of his personal business, including his divorces. He divorced Trudy before he came to Nashville. He brought Jan here with him, so I was there for the divorce between him and Jan, and then Donna Gail. Then there was Sharon Rucker. That wasn't the way it was supposed to be. Harlan was to write the songs, I was to demo and pitch them. I was supposed to be the music man. (After we sold the business to Tree, Harlan married Melanie Smith. He said this was his one true love, and they were still together when Harlan left this world.)

So many funny things happened in the thirteen years I was with Harlan. One time, he wrote a song he thought would be good for Del Reeves. Del had a hit song then, "Girl On The Billboard" (Do da do do do), written by Walter Haynes and Hank Mills. Harlan called Scotty Turner, who was in charge at United Artists (U.A.). He went up and pitched the song to Scotty, who flipped out over it. This was on a Friday morning and he called right then, while Harlan was there, and set up a session for 2:00 PM that day. Harlan came back to the office and left to go fishing at Center Hill Lake for the weekend.

When he got back to the office on Monday morning, he told me, "I'm going to call Scotty and run up there and hear the tape." He was in a hurry, so he stayed in my office and used my phone. The one-sided conversation I heard was:

> "Hello Scotty, just checking to see if you've come into the office yet. I wanna come up and hear Del's session with my song."
> (Pause)
> "You did what?"
> (Pause)
> "What do you mean, you didn't get to it?"
> (Pause)
> "I thought you set up the session to do my song."
> (Pause)
> "Oh!"

I burst out laughing. It seems Del came to the session with a bunch of songs he had found and they did Del's songs but never got to Harlan's.

So, now that the "party was over," and while I was wondering what I was going to do next, Waylon Jennings called me. As life often does, one chapter ends and another begins.

Chapter 16
WAYLON

Waylon Jennings was a big man in the music business, before I went to work for him. He was born in Littlefield, Texas, in 1937. While working as a D.J. in Lubbock, Waylon befriended Buddy Holly. Then Holly produced Waylon's first record, "Jolie Blon," in 1958. Waylon then joined Buddy's band, as a bass guitarist. On the fateful "Winter Dance Party" tour in 1959, Buddy Holly, Ritchie Valens, and the Big Bopper were killed in a plane crash. Waylon married Jessi Colter in 1969. She had the hit, "I'm Not Lisa" in 1975.

Waylon's early days in Nashville were spent with Johnny Cash. The two tore around Nashville drinking and raising hell. They were loaded all the time, kicking down doors, wrecking places, etc. It was hard to ignore half-stoned cowboys dressed in dirty jeans. Country stars were supposed to look like Porter Wagoner and Hank Snow. Waylon just couldn't conform and he was misunderstood. Probably, as he admitted, it was his fault for doing drugs and all that stuff.

Waylon landed at RCA with Chet Atkins as his producer. From the start, Waylon wanted to record his music in his own way, and Nashville's producers resisted innovation. Their way of recording was with a floating pool of sidemen who functioned by moving from studio to studio, recording behind everybody and anybody. These musicians had known each other for years: in the studios, at the Opry, in clubs or in road bands. They anticipated each other's moves. They could work out the backing tracks, improvising arrangements quickly by ear, using number charts rather than reading music, all in a three-hour session. This saved money for the record companies. Chet Atkins, Owen Bradley, or Billy Sherrill could overdub strings, horns, singers, or whatever, once the musicians had put down the basic tracks. Consequently, every record from Nashville seemed to sound like the others, lacking in personality and character, soft and easy listening rather than dancing or drinking music. Chet Atkins knew Waylon was an "outlaw" from the start. Waylon made no secret that he wanted production control of his recordings. That control meant that an artist could name his own producer, or produce records himself, if he wanted. He could pick his own songs and use his road band in the studio, so his records sounded like his true sound, instead of the sound-alike music Nashville produced with session pickers.

Waylon entered into a partnership with Tompall Glaser, who ran a recording studio on 18th Avenue South. Waylon's office was at the Glaser Studios. At that time, the Glaser Studios was the "cool" place to hang out, and it became the major hang-out for the "Outlaws." Waylon and Tompall decided to hold a meeting with Atkins and demand the production control of their sessions. As a result, Waylon and Tompall were allowed a free hand to try to see what they could come up with on their own.

From that time on, Waylon began putting out records that sounded like nothing else in country music. He stripped away all the overdubs, orchestras, and background singers in favor of stark, simple albums of country music. Waylon was not the only one to do this. Willie Nelson left Nashville and went to Austin, Texas, after he had spent a decade in Nashville recording dry runs with Atkins. He found a new recording life in Austin. Tompall Glaser was doing his own style in his own studio.

Hippies, lawyers, and rednecks sat side by side in Texas night clubs, just "diggin'" the music of Willie Nelson and his friends, Billy Joe Shaver and Jerry Jeff Walker. Then, in the early 1970s, the term "Outlaw Music" was given to the music by Willie and Waylon Jennings. In the beginning, radio rarely played their music. Only radio stations in Austin, Texas; Flint, Michigan; and Ashboro, North Carolina were programming what they were calling "Progressive Music" with regularity.

Since Waylon and Willie recorded on the outside of Nashville's "written laws" of recording, the term "Outlaw Music" fit them completely. After all, the word "outlaw" means disregard or defiance of the written law, according to *Webster's Dictionary*.

In Nashville, Jerry Bradley became Chet Atkins's replacement at RCA. He sensed the "outlaw movement" would be a money-maker. Willie was hitting with "Red Headed Stranger." Then, Jessi Colter, Waylon's wife, hit with "I'm Not Lisa." Finally, Bradley realized he might have the hottest thing with Waylon Jennings since Willie. Waylon was booking out as The Outlaws, so Jerry approached Waylon with an "Outlaws" package, consisting of Waylon, Willie, Tompall Glaser, and Jessi Colter. Waylon liked the idea. They finished the recording and got it out in 1976.

Don Davis in the 1970s.

Nobody realized how hot the album, called "Wanted: The Outlaws," would become. It sold to country and rock, pop and easy-listening fans. It was the very first album out of Nashville to go platinum (one million units). They were revolutionaries; the rebels had fought the establishment and the rebels won. The Outlaws kept having hits. In 1976, 1977, and 1978 Waylon had three consecutive hits: "Good Hearted Woman" with Willie, "Luckenbach, Texas" with Willie at the end, and "Theme from the Dukes of Hazard" from the TV series.

Jennings insisted on using his own band, and actually got the right to use his road band in the studio. Nowadays, that might not seem unusual, but it was unheard-of in 1976. The usual procedure was to staff the session with "studio pickers," great musicians, but in Waylon's eyes they were too good, too slick, and too polished. Nashville resisted this innovation, realizing this could put an end to the "patriarchal" Nashville system, meaning those entrenched record executives who had always called the shots might not be using Nashville studios, producers, and session musicians if they found out they could get better records without them.

I was not a stranger to Waylon Jennings. In 1965, Wilderness entered into a publishing agreement with Waylon's Baron Music. Then, in 1966, Waylon and The Waylors recorded an album paying tribute to Harlan Howard's song-writing. They did twelve of Harlan's songs in two sessions, spaced a week apart. They rehearsed the album the night before each recording session in my office at Harlan's, with a small, two-track tape recorder. I helped make the arrangements. Some of the songs had been hits and some had not. One of Waylon's favorites was "Beautiful Annabel Lee." They also recorded "She Called Me Baby," and Waylon said afterwards, "I'm not sure we ever beat the office version of 'She Called Me Baby,' despite all the leakage and phones ringing and general mayhem."

Still, I was surprised in 1978 when Waylon called. He said he wanted me to come to his office and "hang out." By then, he had his own building, a beautiful old house at 17th and Edgehill.

I had heard rumblings and had seen a TV news report about a raid that had been made at Waylon's place looking for drugs. I was a little dubious about going over there, but I went for a couple of days. He said he wanted me to "kinda look things over." Well, okay, but I wondered what he really wanted. I found out he wanted to hire me as his Operations Manager. My primary task, as Waylon outlined to me, was to determine a balance of income and expenditures and to go on the road with the band a week, go to the shows, critique the band, and let him know what I thought. That was alright, I could go on the road and ride the bus.

The band members learned I was going on the bus and joked to Waylon, "We're gonna get him!" Waylon begged them, "Boys, don't do it, bad mistake." I thought how I could pull their leg. Now, I'm a really bad poker player; I'm not even fair-to-middling. When I got on the bus, the first thing I said was, "Hey, boys, I understand y'all play poker on this bus." They nodded, "Oh, yeah, we deal a few hands." The next thing I said was, "You know, I've always wanted to learn how to play poker." They misread my innocent remark. "Ah-ha-ha! Got us a shark here," they said among themselves, thinking I knew how to play! Those guys didn't pull out a deck of cards all week. I really won that hand.

When I got back in town, Waylon asked me what I thought about the show. I was careful how I answered. I told him that the band sounded fairly well, but they all stand in one lump looking at each other when they ought to be playing for the audience.

Jerry Bradley, Mohammed Ali, Connie Bradley, a producer for RCA, and Don Davis.

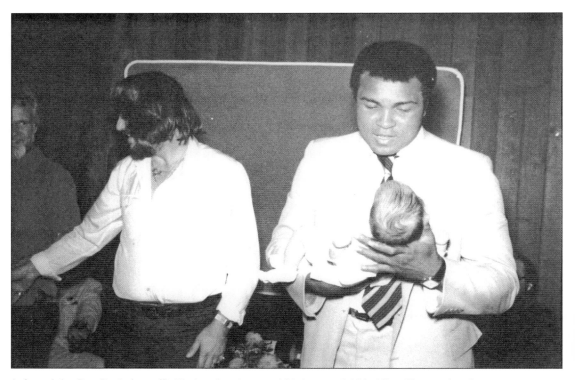

Left to right: Don Davis (cut off), Waylon Jennings, and Mohammed Ali holding Shooter Jennings.

I became Waylon's "social associate" when dignitaries came to town to meet with him, and then he'd disappear. I was left to entertain them and make them feel glad they showed up. One time, Peter Fonda, the actor, had just made a movie with Brooke Shields. They had not yet put music to the movie. Waylon was considered pretty hot then with The Dukes Of Hazard, so Fonda thought it might be good to involve Waylon in the music. Fonda cruised into town and brought a VHS copy of the movie with him. I set up a showing at the Hall Of Fame Motor Inn, in the conference room, and they provided us with a projection TV with a large screen to view the movie. Afterwards, Fonda and I were in my room and the phone rang. It was Mae Axton, a publicist (and part

Waylon Jennings. Photo inscribed, "Don, When I came to Nashville I was penniless but, thanks to you, I now owe $100,000. But you're still in there swinging. Your buddy always, Waylon (Hot Drum) Jennings."

writer of "Heartbreak Hotel" by Elvis Presley). Mae had been in this business forever and was a friend of mine. She asked to speak with Peter. When I told him that Mae Axton wanted to speak with him, he got excited. "Oh, my God, is that really 'Mother Mae'?" He had a long conversation with her. Waylon had said he would see us at the office after we viewed the film, but Waylon didn't show up. I took Fonda to the Exit Inn and showed him around town.

Another time, James Garner came to town and spent the morning with Waylon, who said he had some business to take care of and would be back in a little while; of course, he never returned. I loved Garner's show "The Rockford Files" on TV, and I spent the rest of the day visiting with him. He was most interesting and told me behind-the-scenes stories and antics that I loved.

Then, Mohammed Ali was coming in for Shooter Jennings's birthday. Waylon and Jessi were having a blow-out for Shooter at their house. I was designated to meet with Ali at the airport and set things up, and Waylon ducked out. Ali had an associate, Howard Bingham, with him. Bingham was a photographer by trade, but referred to himself as Ali's Liaison Officer. I picked them up at the airport and took them to the Jennings house where they had a good time. The next morning, Ali wanted to get to Louisville, Kentucky, his home town. He had trouble getting a flight, so I got Waylon's personal bus and driver to take them to Louisville. As a matter of fact, Ali wanted to drive the bus, so I waved goodbye as Ali steered down the highway. (Later, on I saw Bingham on TV at the 0. J. Simpson trial. He was a witness. I was surprised to see him there.)

Jack Thompson taped a show called "50 Years of Country Gold" and hired Robert Urich to emcee the show. I was working with Jack, doing the music. The company we hired to tape the audio made mistakes on the 24 track, so he took the tracks to Youngun Studio. Chip Young had bought the nice studio from Fred Foster of Monument. We had made the original on a remote at the Tennessee Performing Arts Center (TPAC). I picked up the original and took it to Youngun and called in some of the band to re-do some of the tracks. For instance, Waylon was singing, but the bass drum wasn't on the track. One of the guys who was working for us at the studio, was a musician. He got down on his knees with his hand on the bass drum and we put the bass drum back on the tracks in that manner. One of the major problems with the tape was Urich's part. He did some singing, but his singing voice was almost as bad as mine. We had a harmonizer in the studio, and were able to have him re-sing everything. We tuned it up like Perry Como. Urich was really happy. He said, "If I ever sing again, I'm gonna have you come and doctor me up."

When Johnny Cash and Waylon Jennings decided to help George Jones by getting him on a plane to a place to cure his addiction, they were going to bankroll the treatment and it cost a great deal of money. They stuck that problem on me and John and Waylon decided I needed to have a communications beeper. I strapped it on my side and suddenly my life wasn't mine anymore. Anywhere I'd go, that beeper would go off. "Hey, we got George cornered here and you need to get here and see if you can't load him up and get him organized." This went on for several weeks. John and Waylon almost drove me crazy. At one point, they had a jet at the airport with a pilot ready to leave for a treatment center in Birmingham, but we could not corner George. He was really comical. One morning, he showed up at my office and said, "I'm ready to go, Don." Just then the phone rang and I took the call. When I was done, I turned around and said, "Okay, let's go, George." But George was gone! After all this was over, George came by my office. He was driving a canary yellow, stretch limousine and asked if he could borrow my Mercedes for a little while. He was gone for three days. He went to Muscle Shoals, Alabama, and I was left to drive the monster of George's all that time

I was with Waylon for a couple of years. We had a lot of fun times. I was neither an accountant nor a mathematician, but it only took a short time to determine what was going on behind the scenes. Waylon's professional expenses far exceeded his income. I tried to get his problems straightened out. By the time I'd tie one end, another would be coming untied. There were so many money problems. I had to borrow money to put him and his entourage out on the road. Waylon's going price was fifty thousand dollars a night for a seven-day tour. We always got an advance from the buyer for each date, so I'd send them out and they'd come back from a tour with zero funds. The road manager, Tom Bourke, would come in after a tour and my standard question was, "Where's the road money?" His standard answer was, "I'll get it to you," after he hemmed and hawed around. Well, he never did. There wasn't any money. It was all spent.

Neil Reshen was managing Waylon while Reshen's former partner, Mark Rothbaum, was managing Willie Nelson. I reported my findings regarding unnecessary expenses to Reshen, but I was ignored. Meanwhile, I found out that Reshen was borrowing money from the bank, using CDs in the bank as collateral. The CDs were funded with record royalties, and Waylon was collecting a lot of royalties from record sales.

The manager was borrowing a lot of money for the expenses. It got to be that all the record royalties and road work were for nil. Just a waste of time paying a bunch of people. During this time, Waylon was at super star status and I felt his income should have been invested in such a way to protect his future interests. Again, I was unable to get the manager's cooperation. Reshen and I were always at odds. One time, RCA called and wanted me to pick up a platinum album for each of the managers, Reshen and Willie's manager Rothbaum. I did and brought them to the office and called Reshen and told him that his was there. Somehow, he learned I had Rothbaum's, too, and he told me to take it back to RCA and give it to them. I had a better idea. I had found out that Willie was in town staying at the Spence Manor. I called him and took his manager's award to him. Then I had a real problem with Reshen. He was really angry.

Richie Albright, a drummer and band leader, was a business partner in several of the corporations. We were at odds about a lot of expenses. For instance, he was flying truck drivers from Oklahoma City to drive the equipment trucks. Meanwhile, there were truck drivers walking the streets of Nashville looking for jobs. The boys all slept at the best hotels and had king-size beds—everybody, band roadies, and all. Richie was even paying a guy five hundred dollars a week on the road to tune guitars. Expenses on the road were out of sight; there was more money going out than coming in. I signed all the payroll checks and all the checks that went out of that office, so I knew what was going on.

I tried to discuss finances with the manager several times. He refused to deal with any business matters by phone. It happened that manager Reshen was to undergo heart surgery. He asked me to come to his house in Connecticut and he would show me all the details of Waylon's business, just in case anything happened, so I would be able to take over and handle everything. He had a limo pick me up at the airport and drive me to his house. He wined and dined me the whole time I was there; he did everything but take care of business. I went home.

Sometime later, Reshen had a heart valve replacement at the New York University Hospital. Waylon, Jessi, and I decided to go to New York at this critical time, but Waylon was on the road so Jessi and I went ahead and Waylon was to meet us there. Jessi and I settled in at the Waldorf Astoria Hotel to wait for Waylon. I went for a walk, and while I was roaming around I stumbled in on the furrier where June Carter Cash had been buying all her furs. I went in and after I looked around at this mammoth place, I put in a call to Jessi at the hotel. "Put on your walking shoes. I want to show you all of these furs." I walked back to the hotel and met Jessi in the lobby. She was all dressed up and, instead of sneakers, she had on very high heeled shoes. Jessi was not very tall, and as we walked to the furrier she was taking three steps to my one. After a few minutes, she said, "Please, Don, let's take a cab." But we kept on walking, with Jessi click-click-clicking down the sidewalk. When we got there, Jessi went wild. She bought a fur for herself, one for her daughter and one for her housekeeper (on my credit card). She ordered them all monogrammed and shipped to Nashville. Then we walked back to the hotel. Waylon arrived and she told him that I had walked her to death.

After Reshen's operation, he was in the recovery room and the hospital staff would not allow any of us in to see him. I found out the R.N. in charge was from Mobile, Alabama, so I knocked on the recovery room door and spoke with her, giving her my name, rank, and serial number. It turned out, she was from Mobile and she asked me if I was the same Don Davis from the "Alabama Jubilee." After that, we all had clear sailing. We got in, one at a time.

After Reshen recovered, he came to Nashville in March 1980. While he was here, he did not meet with me at any time. From this point on, I realized that something was seriously wrong with the management of Waylon Jennings's assets. Finally, I was having to use my own personal money to get Waylon out on the road. At one time, I put thirty thousand dollars on my American Express card. I even had bills in for Lear Jets. It is disconcerting to get a letter from American Express saying I still owed $23,483.61 on my *cancelled* American Express account. There was money coming in, but it was all going out. They didn't bring back one dollar from any road trips. In addition, taxes were due in the amount of $45,750.

Waylon and his band went to the West Coast to tape the "Waylon" television special. The manager repeatedly refused to forward our operating funds and, because of the high expenses due to the TV taping and ordinary office expenses, again I used my own credit and borrowed almost a hundred thousand dollars from Nashville banks. The manager promised to reimburse me, but he never did. There were times when the operation of Waylon Jennings Enterprises came to a standstill and I knew that Waylon's assets were in jeopardy.

When his total unpaid bills were $1,654,916.57, I decided to tell Waylon and Jessi they were broke. I wanted to go to their house and tell them. Gary Baker was their accountant and I talked with him about it. Gary was an honest, straight-up man. He owned the Fairground Race Track and also had an interest in the track at Bristol, Tennessee. He took care of the accounting for Waylon and I was keeping him informed of the problems. He also knew from looking at the books, just what kind of condition Waylon was in. Gary and I both decided to go out and tell them about it. We met at the office and were getting ready to leave for Waylon's, but somehow Reshen got wind of our plans. The phone started ringing every five minutes. "Do not go out there, under no circumstances are you to go out there and tell Waylon and Jessi about this!" After quite a few phone calls, we ignored the advice and went out and informed them. I knew Waylon was stunned. I told Waylon that I was leaving and that he needed to fire Neil Reshen and probably some others.

Two days after I resigned, I went back to the office to pick up my things. Waylon was there. He said, "Hey, I sent a telegram to Neil Reshen." "Well, hell," I thought. "At last! It's about time!" Then he brought me in a copy of the telegram he sent. It read:

Neil Reshen. Report delivery by phone 6153274625. Neil stop all operations immediately, I mean right now. Don't do one thing for me. I mean anything at all until I call you. You are still my manager but this is all wrong. It has gone entirely too far. At least your health is right. I do understand and I know you cannot get the money. Nothing has changed except you do not take the initiative or do anything for me or my companies unless I ask you to. Do not call me. I will call you later. I mean every word of this. You are not to deal with anyone directly. Listen to me now because I am only going to tell you one time and I expect you to do it. I will do the dealing now. This is also notice to you that you do not have any authorization from this point on to sign my name or act on my behalf for any reason whatsoever. I expect every single word of this to be totally respected and carried out by you. Relax. Waylon

I have kept my copy of Waylon's telegram to this day. When I read it over, it reminds me that Waylon really did respect my ability to call the shots. In essence, Waylon took away Reshen's authorization to sign Waylon's name or act on Waylon's behalf for any reason.

Waylon has since paid me in full for any and all monies I advanced. Rumors began flying on Music Row about where Waylon's money might really have been going, but I didn't make it my business to know anything unless it pertained to business. I didn't want to know. I wanted to keep my hands clean. I tried to know as little as possible. I'd rather just hear the rumors than know what was going on. You know how gossip is, "I heard tell etc., etc." Anyway, a lot of fun times eases the pain of the past and we had a lot of fun times.

The only harsh words I ever had with Waylon were when they all threw a party out at John's house to celebrate their getting well from their bad habits. They invited every human soul that was anybody in Nashville to that gathering and they left Don out. I wasn't invited. That hit me wrong, especially after that deal with George Jones. I got angry. I sat down and composed a letter, called them a heap of bad names, and took it out to John's house. John's brother was on guard duty there that night. I didn't crash the party. I just told him to take that letter to John and Waylon. "I can't leave the guard house," he told me. I said, "You just go on in, I'll stay in the guard house." Waylon and I didn't speak for a little while after that, but naturally everything got all right after a while. I'm sorry, in a way, that I wrote that letter, but in another way, I'm glad I did. I got it off my chest.

Waylon and Johnny would have little falling outs from time to time, and I refereed all those things. I'd go from one to the other, patching things up as best I could. I spent a lot of time doing this between the two of them.

There came a time when the angry outlaw, rebel hero, changed into a clear-eyed, clear-minded artist. He managed to hold onto his marriage with Jessi, even as he fought through the evils that hounded him. As Chet Atkins said, "What a life!" Waylon was the proverbial country boy who rose from unimaginable hardships to attain success and stardom. We all miss him.

Chapter 17
CARNIVAL DAYS

The Disc Jockey (D.J.) Conventions were like a carnival. Life got interesting every fall when the "Carnival," or as some called it the "Circus," came to town. All of us in the music industry (musicians, artists, record companies, publishers, promoters, etc.) waited for them to "send in the clowns." Sure enough, all the D.J.s arrived in town as ready for a party as we were. Don't misunderstand me, we respected those D.J.s; they were very important to the careers of artists, record companies, and song writers. The D.J. is responsible for playing (airing) the records, and the key to the success of a record is the air-play. Demand for the record was created by the D.J. who was the most important bridge between the artist and the buying public.

The D.J. Convention was created in 1952, according to the "official" story from WSM Radio, when a secretary, Marianne Moore (Condra) suggested a convention for disc jockeys. "What better place for them to meet than WSM," she told Jack Stapp, then program director at WSM. Stapp had been looking for a promotional vehicle for the Opry and this seemed like the perfect answer. On the Opry's 27th Anniversary, November 21, 1952, a select 92 D.J.s signed in at the Commodore Room at the Andrew Jackson Hotel on 6th Avenue and Deaderick Street in Nashville.

The first convention was small, a party on Friday night and the Opry on Saturday night. After that, the Convention caught on like wildfire, probably because country music was catching on like wildfire, too. By the second year, D.J.s arrived from all over the world. Record companies rented suites for hospitality rooms and the stars all came in to "howdy" and share drinks. As the convention and the drinking progressed, wannabe artists performed in the hallways, in elevators, and on street corners. Compare this hoopla to a Shriners' Convention or football tailgate parties or a carnival all rolled into one. Let the good times roll!

Radio stations (or promoters) began paying for the D.J.s' travel expenses and the record companies picked up their food tabs and presented lavish showcases. Every breakfast, lunch, and dinner was accompanied by a big show. The D.J.s literally poured into Nashville every fall. It was a wild scene. The old Andrew Jackson Hotel was the official headquarters, but as the years went along, the convention spilled over into every hotel and motel in the area. Records, that had been given for promotional purposes, were sailed out windows as frisbees. Everyone connected with music was there: artists, publishing and record company executives and their cohorts, and an enormous number of fans. Even the locals came to get the free drinks.

I had a legitimate reason to be there. I was always working for an artist, a publisher or a record company. The promotional acts of the famous were almost ridiculous. One year, Col. Tom Parker, who was manager of Hank Snow then, chained a large elephant to a lamppost in front of the Andrew Jackson Hotel. A blanket, across the back of the elephant read, "Thanks D.J.s. Hank Snow never forgets."

Webb Pierce parked his Pontiac convertible (decorated by Nudie with silver dollars embedded on the dashboard, pistols for door handles, and Long Horn steer horns on the grill) in front of the hotel. Nobody ever stole as much as one silver dollar.

The musicians got to poppin' their pills of choice. Old Yellers were the "in" thing at the time. Somebody got the bright idea to substitute cold tablets, which put you to sleep rather than wake you up. They looked like the real thing. I found a D.J. I knew sitting in the hall, on the floor, snoring away. Too many cold tablets!

Pamper Music sponsored a dance one night, with Ray Price's band playing at the Municipal Auditorium. I was going and I got a bright idea. I had a big old Collie dog that had been sick. The vet had given me some yellow vitamin pills to give him. They looked just like the old yellers, even had Simco written across them like the old yellers. The only difference was the size. My dog's pills were the size of a quarter. So, I went to the dance. I knew all the musicians. I flipped one of those pills to the guitar player—whoosh, whoosh—pitched one up to the steel player—whoosh, whoosh! Those vitamin pills tasted just like the old yellers. After all, old yellers were simply vitamins with Dexadrine added. I don't know who thought up the cold tablets, but I admit to supplying the dog vitamins.

Late one night at the convention, Jimmy C. Newman was waiting to catch the elevator. A D.J. got off with a drink in each hand. Jimmy said, "Did you get my new record?" The D.J. managed to slur, "I'sh good to meet you too."

On a Sunday morning, early, after the convention was over, Don "Suds" Slayman, Dale Potter, and I walked through the hotel on our way home; all three of us were hung-over. Suds walked along with an ice bag on his head. I took Suds to his home on Douglas Avenue, in East Nashville. He was married to a stocky girl named Floella. Suds was moaning, "Oh, she's gonna kill me." I told him, "Don't worry about her. Just kick the door open, walk in there, and tell her to get you something to eat." Well, he did what I told him and Floella beat the shit out of him. He never let me forget that.

The not-so-famous had their own promotional gimmicks. One year, Clyde Beavers rode a mule from Georgia to Nashville. Heaven Lee, a stripper from Printer's Alley, was unloaded from the back of a truck on a white horse, fully nude, the Lady Godiva of the Convention. (Police had her back in the truck very quickly.) Some D.J. fell from a hospitality room on the third floor out a window. He hit the canopy below, crawled out, slid down the pole, walked through the lobby still holding his now empty glass, went back to the bar in the same hospitality room, and asked for a refill. His friend said, "Where ya been, good buddy?" "Jes' stepped out for a breath of fresh air," he replied.

Tex Ritter's room caught on fire one year, the only casualty being his wife's clothes.

One D.J. dived head-first off the mezzanine. "How come you didn't stop him?" a friend asked. "I didn't know he couldn't fly," was the response.

Ray Kinnamon and Van Q. Temple, D.J.s from Atlanta, showed up saying they were from the International Broadcasting Co. (IBC). No such company existed! They put a big banner across the front of the Andrew Jackson announcing, "Welcome IBC," which set the stage, and interviewed the most soused fans they could find. Van would say,

This is Van Q. Temple from the IBC. I see a sea of people coming together in a common cause. We have here a participant.

Then he would proceed to interview his selected victim. Later on, all this was put on record. One person, identified as Big Slim, said:

> I was supposed to appear at the Attica State Prison, but I had an attack of laryngitis. Then the prisoners at Attica all rioted because I had to cancel my scheduled appearance.

Then there was the guy who said:

> I actually sat on Jimmie Rodgers lap when I was little. When I grew up I sounded so much like Jimmie nobody would believe I wasn't him. It ruined my career.

They interviewed everybody from the girl-watchers on Broad Street in front of Tootsie's to a man in the bath tub at the hotel. When Ray and Van went home to Atlanta, they put it all out on record. Of course this was hilarious to all of the "in" crowd in the business. I guess the fans who were the butt of the joke never knew about it, as the records were only distributed among the music business "crazies."

At Wilderness, I had posters made that listed all our songs. I hired Billy Swann, with a staple gun, to go all over Nashville putting these posters on telephone poles. The city was plastered with posters for everybody—from the nobodies to the stars.

During these years, Ralph Emery was the host of the All Night Radio Show at WSM. All of us with a record to promote used to take our records up to him to play. In the 1970s, Ralph had a young sidekick, John Riggs, working with him. John also was an aspiring song writer and identifiable by his bald head. Marty Robbins used to go up to Ralph's and stay all night, until 4:00 A.M., playing the piano and chatting with whoever was there. Right before Fan Fair, I heard Marty ask John if he could rent his head. Marty said he would pay John $100 a day if he could rent his head. All he had to do was write the name of Marty's latest record on his head and walk around the Fan Fair celebration for four days at the State Fairgrounds. I'm sitting there thinking, "Will he do it?" John said, "If you're crazy enough to pay that, I'm crazy enough to do it." When Fan Fair began, there was John, walking around with "A Man and a Train" written in lipstick on his head.

The following October, at the D.J. Convention, the first person I saw was tall, bald, John Riggs with "Marty Robbins, CBS Records" written on his head. I said, "John, where is the name of Marty's latest record?" John looked at me as if I was a crazy man and said, "Marty offered me the same deal, but I'll be doggoned if I was gonna put "Love Me" on MY head and walk around among this crowd." Well, I thought, this is better advertising than my posters on the phone poles.

If you were never lucky enough to attend one of these conventions, you missed it all. Think of crowds pressed into small spaces, elevators so crowded you had to walk up and down stairs that were so crowded you had to walk single file. At the end of the convention, the hotel was a wreck. The life-sized portrait of Andrew Jackson looked down on almost total devastation. By Sunday morning, the old hotel resembled a battlefield. No one ever slept during the entire convention. I wish I had thought of the Alka-Seltzer concession when it was over.

Finally, the Andrew Jackson Hotel, built in the 1920s, got too old and the D.J. Convention moved to more modern facilities. I always wondered, if in reality, they threw us out. One day, a demolition team came in and "loaded" the old hotel with dynamite; in fifteen seconds all our memories imploded.

It's over for good now. The CMA and the Grand Ole Opry hold a tame Country Music Week. They celebrate the Opry's birthday with a big cake at the Opry. The D.J.s hold a seminar. The good times don't roll anymore.

Poster for a Jimmie Rodgers concert, 1958.

Part Three
From Nashville to Mobile Bay

*No use wonderin' where I should go
It's on the Gulf of Mexico
It's a honeysuckle heaven
By the name of Mobile.*

—Wells/Holt

Chapter 18
Peace by the Bay

I met my wife, Serilda, in 1985, in Portland, Tennessee. She did not aspire to be a singer or anything else in the music industry. I liked that.

I was still working some then. New York hired me to enhance a bunch of old monaural sessions, split them up, and simulate stereo. I did quite a bit of that type of thing. Then, I just got tired of doing it. I didn't want to mess with anything anymore. I turned on the answering machine; anyone who called thought I was busy and I just didn't get back to them. That's when I decided to leave Nashville and hang up my gloves. I got rid of everything I had to paint or mow.

Serilda and I moved to Gulf Shores, Alabama. My idea was to stay on the beach and just be lazy. I married Serilda in 1990, in Bay Minette, Alabama. The city clerk, who everybody called "Marrying Sam," looked us straight in the eyes and literally sang out, "Do you take this....etc."

I had noted all these people spending a lot of money on weddings, and then six months later "he" would lose his job and "she" would get sick and they wished they had all that money back. Our wedding cost us fifteen dollars and we've been eating steak ever since. We haven't had any lean years. I built a new place down here and we've just been getting along fine. We are living our lives peacefully, down by the Bay.

I got to thinking about when I quit playing a steel guitar and started to work in the business. I suppose young musicians out there are wondering how I could give it up, how I could just quit playing. Well, first I reached a point where I got tired of it all, the packing and unpacking, the traveling, the same old licks. Then, when it got to the point that I'd go out to a Texas honky-tonk and there would be a little young steel player there that made me look sick, I knew it was time to do something else. I had reached my pinnacle. I didn't resent it, and every time I saw one of those aspiring youngsters I'd clap and say, "Go, man, go!" When I reached this certain point in playing, I got so I didn't enjoy it. I just wasn't in love with playing anymore.

Serilda and Don Davis at the Alabama Hall of Fame, 1997.

There was a time when 7-Up and sliced bread were nothing compared to a steel guitar. When I started recording, I thought folks bought all those records just to hear me play. Hank Williams WHO? I actually thought I was bigger than Hank. This is a trap musicians fall into. In reality, records are bought for their "star power."

I decided there were ways to make a living other than playing a guitar. I had been on one side of the glass; I told myself it was time to get on the other side and do better. Harlan's offer couldn't have come at a better time. I was ready for the business side of music.

I have always tried to help young steel players who aren't up with music the way I was. When I was playing local gigs around Mobile, there was a kid named Barney Miller, who used to walk from Chickasaw to Mobile just to hear me play. When I left town to play with Pee Wee, Barney was about twelve years old. One day, he talked to my mother, who asked him, "Barney, would you like a guitar to use? Don left a guitar under his bed. The strings are all rusted. I ain't giving it to you, but you can take it home and use it." Barney took that guitar home and he said, "I truly believed I could play like Don because that guitar had been his." I don't remember what kind of guitar it was, but it was black and had eight strings. When I went home to visit, I called Barney and asked him how he liked my guitar. He said, "Aw shucks, the strings are all rusted and you didn't leave one lick on that guitar." I said, "Okay, I'll just come and get it." Barney was fast to tell me he was just kidding. In fact, he had worked for Jack Lassiter's Wood Shop making clothespins, just to get enough money to buy new strings. In a recent interview, Barney said, "Don showed me all kinds of things like tunings, hot licks, etc." For my part, I was just proud that my guitar had started him off. His first real job was with Dub "Cannonball" Taylor, for $5 a day. Barney went on to become the first steel player to receive the Musician of the Year Award, from the Atlanta Society of Entertainers.

Don Davis's wall of awards, including the Adjutant Generals School certificate.

After I'd been in Nashville for so long, the new kids on the block used to ask me for advice. When Lloyd Green came to Nashville, he asked me what kind of steel guitar he should play. I told him to play whatever he liked. Lloyd thought that to be politically correct, he ought to buy a Sho-Bud. "Not necessarily," I said. "You need to play the guitar you feel most comfortable with." Lloyd, through the years, has become one of our most notable session players, due to his skill at playing licks that fit the singer completely.

Buddy Emmons took up where I left off and improved on it. I say that because he had just come to Nashville when Bigsby built a guitar for me that had no frets. You could tell it was a Bigsby because it had their pick-ups on it. Other than that, there was no telling who made it. I told everybody I didn't need frets and would play it and look around everywhere but at that guitar. It became kind of a comedy act. Everybody laughed at me, including Buddy, who laughed his head off. Emmons plays like that now, seriously. I think he started doing this on his shows because he had seen me and thought it was funny. It does set your act apart. "Look man, no frets!" Emmons is called "Big E" now, and sometimes "Derby Power," for the derby hat he wears. He abandoned the cowboy hat image.

The electric steel guitar gained real popularity by the mid-1930s. Sears Roebuck and Montgomery Ward stores advertised them in their catalogs by then, for $65, and that included an amplifier. The first steel guitar I owned was a Sears, single-neck, 6-string. Next, came a National single-neck, 8-string, and then I had my first double-neck built, a Gibson and National bolted together.

I had all kinds of guitars and I used all kinds of tunings to get different sounds. I'd get tired of one or like another better. I'd get rid of them by giving them away or by selling them. I didn't love any particular instrument, like some steel players do. I didn't have a sentimental attachment to any of them. I just didn't look upon them as my "babies."

I have owned and done away with a lot of guitars: a National double-neck, 8-string; an Epiphone double-neck, 7- and 8-string; a Windham double-neck, 8-string and a triple-neck, 8-string; the Bigsby triple-neck, 8-string, no frets. Then I went to pedals and had three Fender triple-necks, 8-strings, two Sho Bud, double-necks, 10-strings and a Shot Jackson single-neck, 8-string.

Advertisement for Daland Custom Steel Guitar, in *Pickin' and Singin' News*, August 14, 1954.

In 1955, I joined up with Hank "Sugarfoot" Garland and Harold "Shot" Jackson in building a custom pedal steel guitar. We called it the Daland. It was a double-neck, 8-string guitar with two pedals. You see, in 1954, Bud Isaacs had revolutionized the steel guitar by playing a Bigsby pedal, steel guitar on the Webb Pierce record "Slowly." Within a year, everyone in Nashville was trying to imitate that sound. We called it "note-bending" and all the steel players tried all kinds of tricks to copy Isaac's style. Crude set-ups were created out of coat hangers, old gas and brake pedals, you name it.

When we found out how Bud had done it, Shot, Sugarfoot, and I decided we could manufacture as good a guitar as Bigsby. Sugarfoot made and wound the pick-ups. Shot put the pedals on. They were crude, the push-up kind. I designed and had the castings for the tuning keys made by Precision Parts. I also designed and had the bodies made at Kern Antique Reproductions from birds-eye maple. We didn't put a logo on the guitars, as we only made ten of them and we knew they were Dalands. We advertised them in *Pickin' and Singin' News*. This venture only lasted a short time. Sugarfoot was busy with sessions and I was busy with other things and we lost interest. Shot kept on with the idea. He built Howard White a 5-pedal, double-neck, as Shot said, "In my chicken house." Then Shot teamed up with Buddy Emmons and they perfected the "Sho Bud." It became the best-known pedal, steel guitar of its day, eventually adding knee levers and all the "whistles" you see on that guitar today.

Owen Bradley, Gabe Tucker, Slim Whitman, Bob Moore, Hank Garland, Don Davis (back to the camera with his Daland guitar.

Years later, I was in my office at Wilderness Music when an old friend and a steel player, Billy Ray Reynolds, came in and told me he saw a steel guitar upside down in a mud hole outside with the pedals hanging down. He wanted to know why it was out there. I told him I was going to play it one day and I couldn't get the darn thing in tune, so I got mad and threw it out there. But Billy Ray said, "I want it," and I said, "Ya got it!" So Billy Ray took it and that was the last I heard of the last-known Daland Guitar in existence. Recently, I asked Billy Ray about it and he said, "Well, I thought about giving it to the Country Music Hall of Fame because of its history, but finally I gave it to Randy Reinhardt, who is somewhere in Texas."

Sometime later, the oddest thing happened. Christopher Lucker, a senior vice-president at Dolphin Group, Inc., in Los Angeles, wrote me that he thought he had my Daland steel guitar. He sent me pictures from every angle. I was pretty sure it really was my guitar. Then I saw the proof. I had moved one of the necks so the pedals would work better and I left the original holes where the neck was mounted without filling the holes in. Those holes were still there. It was definitely my Daland. When I asked him how he had found it, he said he had bought it from Mike Cass in Dickson, Tennessee. Naturally, I called Mike and he said he had gotten it from Randy Reinhardt in Texas. "In fact," he said, "it was in such bad condition I thought about making a coffee table out of it. When I told Chris Lucker in L.A. about it, Chris told me not to do that, to send it to him." Mike did, and that's the story of my Daland. What happened to the other nine we built? I don't know. Maybe someday another will be found.

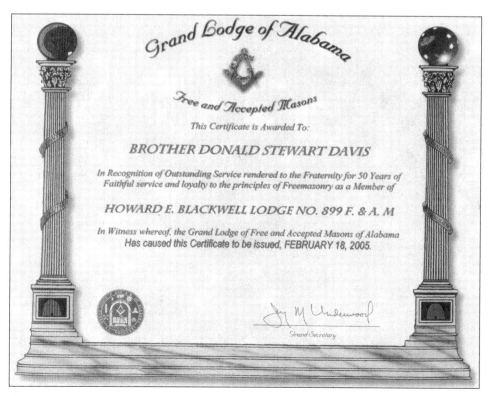

Award from the Grand Lodge of Free and Accepted Masons of Alabama to Brother Donald Stewart Davis, 2005.

One day, I got to looking at a Sho Bud guitar that I had that was sitting unused. I packed it up and took it to Nashville with me. I called Bobbe Seymour, a steel player who also owns a steel guitar business, Steel Guitar Nashville. I told him I had a double-neck, pedal steel I'd like to sell. I told him what I wanted for it and he said, "Is that with a case?" I told him, "No, I'll just bring it to you as it is." Bobbe said, "Now, Don, be sure you pack it good. Every beat-up guitar I ever saw got that way because it was not put in a case to protect it." When I started to take it to Bobbe, I remembered what Bobbe said about protecting it, so I thought, "Oh, ho, one last gag!" Bobbe thought I was still in Gulf Shores. He didn't know I was in Nashville. I set the guitar up, pedals, legs, and everything, then put it in the bed of my pick-up truck and tied it to the sides with a strap or two. I went roaring into Bobbe's place, coming to a screeching halt: Bobbe said, "I looked out my window and saw Don with that valuable Sho-Bud in the back of his truck. I watched him unstrap it and I just knew it would be damaged. I was almost in tears. Don sat it down in my shop, and there stood the most beautiful Sho Bud I had ever seen. Then, I knew Don was up to his old gags. Some pickers never change. I only said, 'Yeah, Don, you really got me!'"

As I was remembering all the circuitous routes I've taken in a life—my time in show business and how lucky I've been—I forgot to mention my song writing "ability." Everyone in Nashville is a songwriter. If you don't believe me, just mention to anyone you meet—the bartender, the waitress, the taxi driver, whoever—that you're in the music business and they will sing you a song they've written every time. I never intended to write a song. I was, first of all, a musician and that enabled me to move on to other projects. However, circumstances sometimes arose that caused me to write a song. I was never a lyric writer, I was a melody writer. Even though my career as a writer was a seldom thing, I do have songs recorded and earning BMI. Right here, I want to thank all my co-writers who wrote the words to my melodies. Danny Dill, a renowned songwriter at Cedarwood Publishing, and I wrote a song titled "Let Me Talk to You." Ray Price recorded it and even used it as a closing song on dances he played. It was also recorded by Waylon Jennings, Mel Tillis, Roy Clark, Wanda Jackson, Art Price, Dottie West with the Jordanaires, the Po' Boys, Willie Nelson, Elton Britt, and Danny Denver. This song became mutually profitable for Danny and me. And then I wrote some less profitable songs:

"Adios Aloha" (with June Carter)
"Bustin' Thru" (with Speedy West)
"Do You Ever Feel This Way" (with John R. Cash)
"I'm Afraid Of The Dark" (with Jimmy Longer)
"I've Got To Get Peter Off Your Mind" (with Glenn J. Jones)
"Little Lies Hurt A Lot" (with Leroy Davis)
"Losin' My Baby Again" (with Danny Dill)
"No Baby, No" (with Ugene Dozier)
"Ridin' On A Freight Train" (with Leroy Davis)
"Ring On Your Finger" (with George Morgan)
"She Made One Mistake" (with Harlan Howard)
"Splidene" (with Robert V. Braddock)
"Take The Hands Off The Clock" (with Leroy Davis)

"Teenage Girl" (with William Berlin and Dan Hoffman)
"You're So Cold I'm Turning Blue" (with Harlan Howard)
"Love Is A Very Strange Thing" (with Harlan Howard)

There are all kinds of music styles and all kinds of approaches to writing songs. Great hits have been written in honky-tonks, on the lake, on the road, at home, and in offices. When the great Blues fiddler, Papa John Creach, was asked how he wrote his music he said simply, "Oh, I just scratch 'em out." I guess I might say of myself, "Oh, I just pick 'em out."

In 1997, I received an unexpected honor. I was inducted into the Alabama Music Hall of Fame at Tuscumbia, Alabama. I was awarded the Alabama Music Hall of Fame Life Work Award for Non-Performing Achievement. I now have my own star in that Hall of Fame, along with other greats from Alabama. Serilda and I were treated royally on the big night when the awards were given out. It all came as a complete surprise to me. In fact, they couldn't find me and had to locate me through Fame Studios in Muscle Shoals.

Country music was so different when I started out. There was no television in the 1940s; it was radio or the movies or nothing. Our records were released on ten-inch, 78 rpm discs. They were played on the radio by a D.J. who actually picked what he wanted to play himself. Fans bought the records they heard on the air for 79 cents or less. Songs were simple and mostly beautiful, often played with three chords and a capo. The beer drinkers in taverns could put their nickels in a juke box to hear their favorite records. A boy and his girl could sit on their front porch swing and make love to the music on their Philco radio. That's when it was all about the music. Life was so simple.

I guess, each generation thinks their music is the best. When you get right down to it, life is a fabric of memories. Some memories are sad and some are happy, some are funny and some are painful. While country music can capture the good times better than any other type of music, it also describes utter loss and desolation better. "Three chords and the truth" is how Harlan Howard described it.

Waylon Jennings' employee identification card, 1984.

There comes a time when each generation settles back and decides to pass on what we learned in the four or five decades given to us. We had to learn on our

Don Davis, 2011.

own and have forgotten sometimes where the creek originated. We just pass on the water and the young hopefuls are thankful for that water. The musicians today are more educated and have much more training than my generation did. They have so much to give to this business. Their talent is not the problem. The way I see the trouble with the music business today is that there is no fun in it anymore. There are no characters around for the laughs. It's all business.

My daughter, Lorrie, once said, "Dad makes life interesting for us when we are with him. His glass is always full and when we are with him, our glasses are full too."

I've always believed that if you're not having fun, you're not doing your job. I've had more fun in this business we call music than the law would allow, and if the law had known they might not have allowed it. My tours along the roads to Nashville and from Nashville to Mobile have been the greatest of times.

I have absolutely no regrets about leaving Nashville. Serilda and I enjoy our life here. I loved the music business the way it was. Yes, it's changed, but change is inevitable. I have accepted change. If we use change to our advantage, it becomes an ally rather than an enemy. I live by the Willie Nelson theory:

> Remember the good times. They're smaller in number and easier to recall.
>
> Don't spend too much time on the bad times. Their staggering numbers will be heavy as lead on your mind.

There's a million and one stories in Music City about all those musicians and singers who have worked the road, those who have made the records, the ones who have written the songs, and the many who have been associated with them. They have all earned their place in country music's history. All of us—the good, the bad, and, most of all, the lucky— have paid our dues in this business we like to call "Music."

Don and Serilda Davis.

AFTERGLOW

To Don from your co-writer:

There stands the bottle,
here's to absent friends.
Here's to all the gals you knew
and to heaven when you die.
If you want to trust somebody,
raise your glass now to Don,
good ole boy still standing.
He's a stand-up guy!

—Love ya, Ruth

Recording Sessions Remembered

Artist	Recorded at	Recorded by	Month/Year
MINNIE PEARL	Nashville	WSM Radio Bullet	1946
DELMORE BROTHERS	Nashville	WSM Radio	1946
PEE WEE KING	Chicago	RCA	Dec., 1946
CLIFF CARLISLE	Chicago	RCA	Dec., 1946
COWBOY COPAS	Cincinnati	King	Dec., 1946
VARIOUS ARTISTS	Cincinnati	King	Dec., 1946
ELTON BRITT	New York		Feb., 1947

Hollywood, California, 1947

Following are just a few of the artists with whom I recorded before the union went on strike on January 1, 1948. Unknown artists were being recorded just so the record companies would have product "in the can."

TEX RITTER
GENE AUTRY
KEN CURTIS
EDDY KIRK
EDDY DEAN
BING CROSBY
TED LEWIS
MARGARET WHITING
JIMMY WAKELY
BUDDY COLE
DINAH SHORE
SOUND EFFECTS
FOY WILLING
JOHNNY BOND
SEVERAL ARTISTS, Lee Gillette, Producer
PAUL WESTON "STARLIGHTERS," Chesterfield Supper Club
HANK PENNY
MILO TWINS

Artist	Recorded at	Recorded by	Month/Year
HANK WILLIAMS	Castle Studios	MGM	Mar. 1&2, 1949

Artists with whom I recorded at Castle Studios between 1949 and 1950:
- ERNEST TUBB
- JIMMY WORK
- ONIE WHEELER
- EDDIE CROSBY
- HANK GARLAND
- CAROLINA COTTON
- HANK WILLIAMS
- FOLEY SISTERS
- LEON PAYNE
- JOE ALLISON
- JIMMY DICKENS
- RED SOVINE
- TEXAS RUBY
- KENNY ROBERTS

Artist	Recorded at	Recorded by	Month/Year
ANITA CARTER	Nashville, Brown Radio Productions	RCA	Aug. 23, 1950
ANITA CARTER	Castle Studios	Columbia	Dec. 10, 1952

Artists with whom I recorded at Bradley Studios between 1953 and 1956:
- PORTER WAGONER
- GRADY MARTIN
- SLIM WHITMAN
- CHET ATKINS
- DAVE RICH

Artist	Recorded at	Recorded by	Month/Year
ANITA CARTER	RCA Studios	RCA	Oct. 26, 1955
ANITA CARTER	RCA Studio	RCA	Nov. 29, 1955
NITA, RITA & RUBY	RCA Studios	RCA	Jan. 25, 1956
ANITA CARTER	RCA Studios	RCA	Mar. 4, 1956

Artist	Recorded at	Recorded by	Month/Year
ANITA CARTER	RCA Studios	RCA	Oct. 25, 1956
GEORGE MORGAN	Castle Studios	Art Satherly, Columbia	Apr. 13, 1949

"Room Full Of Roses" was recorded on this session.

GEORGE MORGAN	Castle Studios	Art Satherly, Columbia	Aug. 26, 1949

"Ring On Your Finger" that I wrote, recorded on this session.

GEORGE MORGAN	Castle Studios	Art Satherly, Columbia	Nov. 7, 1949
GEORGE MORGAN	Castle Studios	Art Satherly, Columbia	Feb. 3, 1950
GEORGE MORGAN	Castle Studios	Art Satherly, Columbia	July 31, 1950
GEORGE MORGAN	Castle Studios	Art Satherly, Columbia	Nov. 24, 1950
GEORGE MORGAN	Castle Studios	Don Law, Columbia	Dec. 6, 1952
GEORGE MORGAN	Castle Studios	Don Law, Columbia	Mar. 30, 1953
GEORGE MORGAN	Castle Studios	Don Law, Columbia	Mar. 31, 1953
GEORGE MORGAN	Castle Studios	Don Law, Columbia	Sep. 1, 1953
GEORGE MORGAN	Castle Studios	Don Law, Columbia	Jan. 7, 1954
GEORGE MORGAN	Castle Studios	Don Law, Columbia	Sep. 8, 1954

Two sessions were done on this day.

GEORGE MORGAN	Bradley Studios	Don Law, Columbia	Jun. 24, 1955
GEORGE MORGAN	Bradley Studios	Don Law, Columbia	Mar. 29, 1956
GEORGE MORGAN	Bradley Studios	Don Law, Columbia	Oct. 16, 1956

I also did sessions in Atlanta for RCA.

INDEX